# You May Already Have What It Takes

## The Art of Winning

# You May Already Have What It Takes

## The Art of Winning

Alante' Adams

Sambouie LLC Publisher

Sambouie LLC Publisher

Sambouie.com


Author: Alante' Adams
Title: You May Already Have What It Takes The
Art of Winning
ISBN: 978-0-9990671-0-9

Author's Photo by:

Sambouie LLC

# Table of Contents

# Foreword

In this book Alante' gives you play by play details and the necessary tools needed for your success.

Not only does he share with you exactly what's holding a lot of people back from achieving their goals and dreams but he also explains exactly what you must do to overcome them so you can start winning in your life.

This book is a must read for all ages.

Kyle "The Dream" Vidrine
Speaker & Author of Wake Up The Winner In You
www.thedreaminspires.com

# Acknowledgments

I am grateful for all my family and friends; I can't pay you guys back with all the money in the world. I would like to give a special shout out to: Helen Ayim, Aaron Adams, Kendra Adams, Lorraine Payne, Edward Payne, Lacoya Thomas, Ileyah Thomas, Aaron Adams Jr, Clifton Adams, and Dr. Wilson. I would like to thank my father for encouraging me by helping to develop this philosophy. My mother for all her support. I want to thank my Grandmother for editing this. I would like to thank my girlfriend for believing in me and insisting that we self-publish. I want to thank my grandpa for his words of encouragement. I want to thank Clifton Adams for always telling it like it is. I want to thank Lacoya Thomas for always thinking business minded. I want to thank my big brother for being the perfect big brother. I would like to thank my niece for winning the writers award at school. It gave me motivation. I am thankful for all the people I went to college with and whom I've done business with. Thank you, Dr. Wilson, for your critiques of my undergraduate writings. I am forever grateful.

# Introduction

**A good book is a book that makes you think; regardless if you agree with the author or not. -Alante' Adams**

Have you ever doubted yourself? You may already have what it takes, but first you must know yourself. Many people are in their heads, but do not know their selves. I stumbled upon these concepts that helped myself and many others know themselves. You are the captain of your fate. This book will teach you how to teach yourself by guiding you from the inside. This guide will empower you to tap into the hidden jewels you have within you. A lot of books cover goal setting and tells you to be yourself. They don't tell you how to be your best self by building your character to win.

People do things for their parents, friends, and money. They never ask themselves the simple questions. For example, "How to be truthful to themselves?" If you can be open-minded about these special concepts and be led by them you will be a winner for yourself. You will discover many ways to win. This book will guide you when you need guidance. This book if used properly will set you free from doubt.

I have studied tons of books while earning my undergraduate degree in Electronics Engineering Technology. I have sacrificed the time and effort to learn these concepts. These concepts that I figured out after bumping my head started to become a formula. To understand this formula you need to know the basic elements that make it up. This book is a new way of thinking once you acquire the basic thought patterns you will be able to peek inside the wonders of your mind and what it can achieve. Accomplishing many of the things I wanted to accomplish may seem different from what somebody else wants? Not everybody wants a $300.00 pen. Who am I to judge? If you apply these concepts you can achieve anything *you* want. A part of finding out what you want is knowing these basic thought patterns.

Everybody will have a different answer when you apply these special concepts. This book is not a one size fits all book. It will help you to help yourself. After you're done with this book your way of thinking will propel you to feel confident enough to be a go-getter. Placing all these hours into studying books, people, and history caused me to have the desire to reach out to others. Your life matters so handle it with care. I see you have the potential to be a go-getter already by picking up this book. A lot of people don't read the introduction. Congratulations.

Many people have small successes in life, but they don't know how to duplicate them. Sometimes when you need to get something done you rise to the occasion, but you don't know how to keep that energy steady. These messages revealed inside needs to be studied over and over to get it inside your spirit. It is amazing how many people read something one time and say they know it. This book will strengthen your brain power like an exercised muscle. The more reps you do the better. It is as simple as that. This is not your conventional advice; I'm not trying to be your parents and buck you up. You must be tough inside to accept these messages. If you're not a person who wants to learn drop this book now.

Be careful if you're reading it just for fun because the awakening you will spark may make you fortunes. These messages are mental stimulation for the brain. People do drugs to alter their perceptions. This is better than drugs that alters perception because this will benefit you. When you feed your mind with this book you will alter your perception of the world around you. This will make you see opportunities you could not see before because of your changed perception. Use this book with care to help guide you on this new high of a fulfilling life. You are on your way to tapping into these powerful messages.

# Chapter 1

## Core Values, Principles, and Purpose

### "If you don't stand for something, you fall for anything." - Dr. Martin Luther King

You must have a belief system that you follow that steers you away from bad outcomes. This belief system must bring you closer to the things you desire. What do you desire? Most people don't know what they want. For example, a child may want something sweet and prefers to eat candy all day. If the child understood the consequences of their candy eating habits they would steer clear of the candy. If they know that the candy brings cavities, toothaches, and painful dental visits, they would reconsider. They would understand that they do not *want* that. Fast forward to adults there is constantly things that grab our attention and it seems like we want whatever it is, but do we really want that? We may reconsider.

Your Core Values, Principles, Purpose, and Vision helps define what you want regardless of the short-term sweetness. Values are what you deem important in your life. Core Values are the five most important values that defines what you stand for. Core Values helps you to make decisions that will benefit you. Core Values guide you like a sail on a boat towards positive long-term consequences and gets you closer to the things you desire. Core Values are your day to day guiders on how to behave in certain circumstances by helping you make decisions that determines your action steps. It is the values that you prioritize when making important decisions or seemingly trivial decisions. Core Values are values such as family, respect, peace, and friendship, et cetera. Without knowing what you value in life your ship can end up off course because life is constantly changing like the weather. You don't steer the same on a beautiful sunny day as opposed to a thunder storm.

Your core values must fit inside your principles like a glove. Principles are concepts you believe in deeply regardless of the circumstances. Your principles are like your rudders on the ship. For example, you can make the right turn with the steering wheel which is the same in life as the right decision, but you can still be heading in the wrong direction. The reason is because if you have core values without principles you would have a disconnect between the steering wheel and the rudders. When the steering wheel and the rudders are disconnected the ship will continue to be at the mercy of the weather because it has no control of the direction it is heading. Principles are laws by which you abide by personally. Principles are rules in your personal game. Examples of principles are I will not lie, I will not be afraid of people, and I will never give up. Principles makes sure you stay on course by acting as boundaries so that you stay on path to reach your goal. If you're ever in a situation where you have to break your principles you know that you are off path. You cannot really break your principles; you break yourself on the principles. Your principles are your indicators that let you know you've made the wrong or right turn. Principles is your personal definition of right and wrong regardless of the external pressures of the circumstances. Once you established your core values and principles you will be closely aligned to finding your purpose.

The purpose is the overarching theme of your life; it is your destination regardless of time. It is your engine and your anchor. Your purpose is the computer that runs the machines. Your purpose is less visible to the world of people. People may be able to see why you made your decision based on that particular circumstance and your core values after close observation. People may guess about your principles, but it is almost impossible for them to see your purpose. Your purpose is naked to the human eye. Your purpose is within you. Only you know for sure your strengths and weaknesses and what makes you unique to reach your goal. Don't start from finding out your purpose. Start with figuring out your core values, next your principles, then your purpose.

Your core values are mostly found by asking yourself why you made your last five decisions regardless of external pressures from friends, family, and your enemies. Your principles come from your unique life experiences and from seeing the people that you don't want to become. It comes from knowing the things you don't want to be. Finding your principles can mostly stem from the "I don't want" category of your life. Experiencing life will help you develop your rudders. The more icebergs the captain sees and successfully dodges or fails to dodge will make them competent to know and understand how to maneuver around most of the problems of life.

When people abide by their principles in life they will develop more confidence in their character and what they stand for. This will help them to become grounded. Character gives them a platform to grow which inevitably leads to their purpose. Core values saves you from burning tons of energy trying to gamble at life for the things it seems like you wanted in the moment. The child is deceived by the sweet stuff because it seemed like that was what they wanted. When it comes to making decisions you don't wonder asking yourself, "What will I get out of the deal?" If you know what your values are you would know what you're trying to get out of the deal. Your principles alone will keep you from negative situations by knowing what to avoid.

Your purpose would let you know when something is your enemy rather that's other people's principles, opponents, or your own personal weaknesses. By having a blueprint which consist of your core values and principles you're already prepared to avoid 99% of the things that's not aligned with your purpose. Your core values and principles make up your ship. As long as you stay on this ship your protected from drowning. You're safe from sinking because your steering is in you not on you. You will become to know who you are and why you're not them. Luke 11:23 says, "He who doesn't worketh with me worketh against me." If you don't know what you're working towards you don't know what is working against you. If I asked you, "Where are you going?" And you simply don't know; well it makes no sense to walk. When you don't know where you're walking at all you don't know what you are walking into; it could be death. You could be putting yourself at risk. Sun Tzu said, "Do nothing that isn't of benefit to you." Avoiding the negative is half the battle. By defining your core values and principles it will help you to avoid the sleep walking zombies in life and help you not to become one. If you don't know the benefits of doing something do not budge. Everything in life you do should be designed towards achieving your purpose. If not you shouldn't move! When a train starts it has a destination it sets out on. If that train moves without knowing where it's going and when it's going to stop that puts everybody at danger including itself; because it is heading for self-destruction. It is like reckless people that don't have any core values, principles or purpose. If you don't have a purpose you're going to fail. Most people end up in the poorhouses because they don't have any purpose. If you were an insurance agent would you insure someone who is reckless?

People who have core values will be able to make the best decisions regardless of their emotions. Emotions are what makes us human; there is no shame in that. Humans should not let their emotions control them, but learn how to use their emotions for them instead of against them. The emotions they attach to achieving their purpose should be more important in their life than emotions in the moment. This will help them to be able to evaluate their actions during an emotionally driven situation. Placing more weight in the emotions of achieving their purpose will let them know when their emotions in the moment will lead them to make a wrong decision. By placing more value on the emotions of achieving their purpose they will know when they are drifting further away from achieving their purpose. When their emotions in the moment are in alignment with the emotions of achieving their purpose they will know when to act boldly. Letting their emotions work for their purpose is the key. If a person wanted to lose weights they wouldn't be eager to stop at a fast food restaurant. They would be so emotionally attached to their purpose of losing weight that they wouldn't want any fast food. When they truly value their purpose they would eat healthy home cook meals and ignore the cravings in the moment.

The purpose in your life is like your North Star that makes sure you have a beneficial productive life that is on course. While circumstances are constantly changing your purpose lets you know instantly what to do to get the best out of each situation rather limiting losses or winning big. I know people that can be of value to others and themselves and have everything it takes to be of benefit to society. They have the best engine on their boat, but they don't know it because they don't see the value in it. Without a purpose that keeps that engine moving it rusts. Someone who sees the value in their engine will buy it from them and they would sell it without thinking twice because they don't see the value in their own engine. It is like that job that pays so little because people are willing to sell their services for cheap. The company recognizes that their engine is valuable for its purpose. Fast Food restaurants love when you don't have a purpose. For example, if you pass by a restaurant, but didn't cook anything you're bound to pull into the drive through and spend at least $15. If you would've prepared a home cooked meal you would have saved money and your health. If you don't have a purpose for your money these fast food restaurants will take your money in exchange for unhealthy, but fast food.

The people or companies with the purpose will continuously take your money because you don't have a purpose for how to spend or invest it. If you don't have a purpose you don't have a defense against people with nefarious purposes. You will be shark bait. A purpose is your objective in life. Your purpose in life is just like a heart vital to achieving success. A person who doesn't work out to keep their heart healthy heart grows weaker. Then it can't pump blood efficiently which causes blood clots and their heart can't perform its purpose, so the person eventually suffers a massive heart attack. Your core values are like your body systems; they work together to make sure that you're functioning properly. The core values help make sure you're on track with your principles. Every core value has a purpose, but if that smaller purpose continuous to get overlooked you will start to lose your proper functioning.

We are humans with emotions and basic needs. People understand that everyone needs money. They understand that money is necessary to life as oil is to an engine. Your engine is like your energy, talents, and abilities. People are satisfied when companies supply oil to their engine. They let the company use their engine because they have no purpose for it. It only feels good that it is filled with oil; therefore, they work their engine for someone else's purpose. This is a reason why people are feeling misused, depressed, and fed up with life. They never find out that it's the leeches that are using their engine to fulfil their needs. People without a purpose are satisfied with getting a little oil because they don't know what to do with their engine. All they know is that they need oil. They miss out on all their benefits because they want just enough to get by. Without the proper core values that lets you know what kind of oil your engine need it could get worst. Without knowing who you are first you don't know what kind of engine you have and what oil it needs. That's why you must know who you are so that you can give and receive proper service. You have to know your own service manual. You have to know your value. You have to start by knowing your core values. We cannot afford to miss out on using that powerful engine that will make you happy and fulfilled. Everybody has gifts and talents that needs to be maintained properly without the right treatment you could blow that engine. Which leads to the poorhouse or worst death. Your engine in jail would be used for the government's purpose which is cheap labor. Don't be a fool to let someone misuse your engine.

It is vital to establish your core value criteria. This will make sure you aren't getting misused by family, friends, or associations because you would stand for something. Your core value criteria will let you know when to abandon the relationship or continue it. It will be a tool to evaluate your relationships of all kinds. Every new year people set goals and don't finish them. Why? Because their purpose was seasonal; they weren't emotionally attached enough to their New Year's resolution to cause them to develop core values and principles. Core values and principles makes sure their ship doesn't stay at the dock but reach their destination. So, without a purpose your engine will be going off emotions and money. Until someone a person "trust" puts the wrong oil in their engine and rocks their boat. Then, they'll become mad at the world because someone put the wrong oil in their engine. By having a purpose, you would start to blame everything that happened to you on yourself. You would start to realize that you're the captain of your ship and there is nobody else to blame if it sinks. You must watch over your talents like a cherished engine and make sure it develops and perform better. You have to water your own seeds in your garden. You can't just set a goal and don't have core values and principles to let the captain know if you're on or off course. Having core values stops you from being unnecessarily emotional and making the wrong decisions because of the sweet stuff. The next time something sweet comes up you would see the poison on the wrapper. You would be so aware of the candy that you start to recognize the package. You will be able to identify the wickedness from a mile away. If I know I wanted to be fit I don't just say, "Fast food is okay every now and then." No, I say, "It is poison." Do you put diesel in your engine if it tells you unleaded only? No! People and companies with purposes that are not aligned with yours will make you say, "Well sense I didn't cook anything and the kids are hungry we might as well stop at the fast food joint." $35 dollars later you're thinking to yourself, " Man I should've planned and prepared my meals for the whole week for that much." After the fast food joint advertisements tempts you by telling you that you can have it your way you're working only to put oil in that company's engine because you're supplying the money it needs. They know you don't have principles to filter out temptation before it gets to you. There is saying called, "Garbage in, garbage out. If you put garbage inside of you there will be garbage to come out of you. If you don't protect yourself from these temptations you will fall victim over and over. For example, a person who tells themselves when the casino gives them free tokens and free liquor that, "Hey, at least it's free, there is no risk." They don't understand the purpose of that casino. The purpose of the casino is to bring you inside. It doesn't care what it has to give away because it knows once your inside you will become tempted. The only way to beat out temptation is to stay away from it. They know you don't have any filters like core values and principles. Another example is the state lottery where the government tells you can't gamble privately, but the government can publicly. You tell yourself, "The lottery ticket is only two dollars." You don't understand the government's purpose. They want all the citizens to think, "It's only two dollars." So that everybody buys a ticket and make the tax revenue bigger. You must put your guard up so that you can filter this garbage out. This will protect you from being misused.

People think they can dock their boats for "free" because they don't have a purpose to go anywhere. People even dock their engines by their mom, pops, and grandparents thinking they are "saving". They're not saving anything they're only using up other people's resources because somebody else is putting oil in their engine. The people who are letting them dock their boats for "free" are the ones who gets the engine problems. The engine problem is called stress. Stress can shut any engine down. The Bibles says, "One bad apple spoils the whole bushel." Once you let people anchor their boat without cost they will suck up your oil like a leech. You have to watch out for people with no core values, principles or purpose. They will kill your engine as well as their own. It is not an option. They will either end up dead, in jail, or killing you and not just with a bullet, but with stress. People who depend on people and the government for oil without work will be a leech. They will always sink the ship. Let's create your core values so that you become great! If you don't somebody will have a purpose for you that makes them great at your expense. Take care of yourself by putting your life on auto-pilot by not constantly having to deal with petty day to day things that try to misuse you. Don't put unnecessary mileage on your engine. This will help you save energy and fuel for your own flight. You must know who you are first to help someone help themselves. To seek others and lift each other up you guys have to have similar principles and shared values that align you all. If not you will never have meaningful and valuable friendships and relationships that can be mutually beneficial. If people skip this step they wouldn't be able to know how to develop a team of people that want to see them succeed because they don't know what they want and who they are. They don't even know how to work with other people's engines to build an empire. What do you do with people with no purpose? Make sure you're protected from them because they can crash into your ship and cause you to sink. They are the clowns at the party who does something crazy that ruins it for everybody. There is nothing you can do about them. Their engines are totaled. They can only help themselves. You have to let the poppers pop and the breakers break.

Vision is your mentor for your purpose. It is your purpose counselor; it helps to make sure your purpose is heading in the right direction. It is your light in the darkness. It says in the Bible, "Where there is no vision, the people perish." Your vision must stay clear of debris so that your purpose won't crash on the sharp rocks of defeat. Vision sees beyond your circumstances into the big picture. It looks at the holistic mapping of your life. Without it you don't know when you're lost. You can have the ambition for your purpose, but without the vision you couldn't see how your purpose results are being manifested. You can be accomplishing your intentional purpose, but wouldn't be able to see the damage your purpose is creating. You wouldn't know when to tweak your purpose if it's misguided. A lot of people believe they have figured out their purpose or calling, but don't have the vision to see how their purpose will realistically be carried out. They are operating without a guidance light. They feel they have a certain gift and talent and assume that is their purpose, but without a vision they will be in the dark and that same gift and talent used by the wrong people can end with people disillusioned, depressed, and worst dead.

Vision is the ability to imagine and visualize before something takes place. Napoleon Hill said, "If a man can conceive he can achieve." You must first be able to see into your vision before you can achieve it. If you don't see the ending you wouldn't know how to start. People have the spirit of procrastination because they don't know how or where to start, but if they had the vision the mind will dream until it comes up with a plan. The subconscious mind is so powerful; dreams, visualization, and imagination are all keys to keeping your vision sharp. Albert Einstein said, "Imagination is more important than knowledge." You have to first be able to think outside of the normal way of thinking by the average who don't tap into their vision. Leaders have the vision. The CEO's are supposed to have the vision. People won't amount to nothing if they don't have vision. People who don't have vision are only good for following. How much worst is it if they are following the blind? They are following somebody else's vision, but cannot see what it is manifesting. Adolf Hitler created a vision for the people of Germany, that led to the slaughter of millions of people and World War II. German citizens embraced the hype that somebody else's vision had created. In during that hysteria the German citizens participated in acts that they are ashamed of because they got caught up in the hype. Do not get me wrong. There is nothing wrong with following someone else's vision. As long you make sure it matches your core values, principles, and purpose. If not do not tarnish your core values, principles, and purpose to join in someone's else vision.

Entertainment like television creates visions for people by using actors, rappers, magicians, et cetera. Their role is to create visions. People are glued to watching them perform imagining that the performers were them. Instead of being the vision and finding their purpose they get sucked into somebodies' else's vision making them rich and the television producers as well. Every action has a reaction and if people don't have a vision behind their actions they'll lose every time. Vision can be blurred because the person's purpose is not keeping it sharp. One way to keep the vision sharp is to read. Vision must be constantly energized. Things that energize the vision is music, healthy relationships, and exercise. There was an old story about a man who ripped his eyes out because his eyes were getting him into trouble. He was not seeing the whole picture. He was always distracted by eye-candy; he wasn't using his mind. Practice to meditate to be able to see the whole picture.

The vision ponders on life. The vision's main purpose is to be forward thinking and anticipating change. The vision anticipates and sees beyond to feed the true purpose. How do you know your vision is functioning properly? You would have this powerful feeling, energy, and motivation to head towards your light regardless of your fear. Fear slows the energization of your vision. Fear of failure, fear of success, and fear of death; you name it. All causes the vision to go dim. Once the vision goes dim the purpose becomes a lost cause. The disillusion starts when you believe once you find your purpose that is the end. People believe that once they figure it out they have graduated from life. They want the pats on the back and congratulations, but wonder why they aren't happy. The vision is progressive; it's the enjoyment of the process. The vision is your natural rhythm. No one else can latch on to your uniqueness. Your vision should be so big you're never satisfied with pats on the back. If the people can see your every move before it happens that is no sign of a big vision. Your vision should happen at your pace. It should be always conquering people's perception of you. Your vision will cause others to want to follow your lead. Your vision should cause things to change for the better. Your purpose will start to manifest. Everything will be in alignment. You will be internally happy that you're on the energized path to fulfillment.

# Chapter 2

## Everybody Can't Hang

### If you're just chilling you will never be great
### -Alante' Adams

Life is made up of people. Understanding human nature will play a big part in the practical side of fulfilling your purpose. First by knowing who you are that is half of the battle. When you know who you are and what you stand for you know what type of people that will benefit you. George Washington said, "It is better to be alone, than in bad company". The reason you cannot hang with everybody is because everybody will not be built with the internal compass of core values, principles, purposes and vision. Everybody haven't figured out their purpose. This can cause them to hang around you once you discover your purpose. People will become attracted to you because it feels you have a direction and people like people who they feel know where they are going. But be aware of the people that want to be like you; dress like you, talk, and walk like you. They have no purpose they may be jealous and want to replace you. Although it may seem flattering to have "yes men" in your sphere of friends get rid of them they are only blocking your vision are worst trying to destroy it.

You must be able to hire slow and fire fast. Which means the hiring of people in your life takes time. It is a process like your vision. They must be able to reach your qualifications, standards, and probation period. The qualifications to reach your team must not be compromised. If you have certain qualifications to enter your sphere of friendship do not lower them. Your vision of what you want will let you know the type of people that are qualified to share a part in it. For example, in a manufacturing environment with machines to produce goods. There are safety guards to cover the motor drive chains. The metal safety guards job is to protect the worker's hands or clothes from getting jammed into the motor drive chain. But what if a person with no vision asks, "I don't even know why they got this here?" Then, takes it upon themselves to move the "bulky thing" and somebody gets their hand jammed in the machine because there wasn't a safety guard covering the motor drive chain. Your qualifications are like that safety guard it protects you from future damages. You must put people through the test to see if they qualify to be in your life. First, they must reach your qualification requirements. Then, they must reach your standards. A standard is a specific level to reach. Your standard criteria should evaluate their core values, principles, and habits. They must behave by a code. A frequent problem that happens when it comes to blurring the vision is when people stop evaluating people. They cut out their qualification requirements. They let anyone into their lives. Your qualifications and standards is your defense mechanism. It keeps the viruses and cancers out. Without it you will not be healthy enough to achieve your purpose. Some people can come into your life and make you sick. When you have to reject people from being in your life it is nothing personal; they don't have the qualifications. There are other people they can hang out with just not you. They could be a top company like you, but you might be in a different industry. You may be heading in a different direction. You must keep around you people that fit your qualifications. If they start to slack you have to be able to fire them fast. That's right; fire them from your life. Fire the people who are the cancers; slackers, naggers, and the haters. You don't have to keep supporting them; they are leaches. They're sucking your vision's energy. Next thing you know you will have no more juice because you're drained by the people that you're around.

You're the result of the five people you hang around the most. Be careful who you associate with because people will influence your mind and your vision. Beware of the "just chillers" because if you're just chilling you will never be hot. This means you will never be great. You will never have the hot hand. If you don't have "get up" you become a slacker. "Just chilling" will keep you at the bottom where there is plenty with no vision lights on. You're a special being with abilities that are untapped, but you can't do it alone. You need people because isolating yourself is not the answer. Learn to prospect for the next best person or people that can help your vision. Always be willing to recruit to your team. When a person on your team core values or principles change and they're not in alignment with yours let them know, "Hey, I'm sorry, but I got to let you go." If you really want to make it to your purpose you would understand that everybody can't come with you to your destination; it's nothing personal. That is why you hire them into your life slowly put them through the test of time before you commit fully to protect yourself from always having to fire.

Not everybody will be made of the same material you are. You have to understand that liking a person has nothing to with achieving your purpose. Sometimes you might have to turn enemies to friends and friends may turn into enemies. If you were upfront about where you were going and you made it clear your qualifications and standards you're just fulfilling your word. You want to take out the guesswork by following the policy of written qualifications and standards. If they drop below the standards let them know and if you see no improvement move on. Part of the reason people stay below their dreams is because they are scared to get rid of the leaches. The power of screening is amazing. It can save your vision, purpose, and life. Do not let anybody bring negativity in you sphere of influence. Protect your vision by monitoring your associates constantly. Re-evaluate who you hang around closely. You have the chance to select your team with precision. Everybody who gets a position on your team earns it. Not because you personally like them which may cause future problems when or if you don't. You bring people in your life who will help you achieve your vision with a win/win solution. I can't stress enough the power of rejecting people and firing them. They will be okay, but by knowing what you expect they won't come around and ruin your vision. They could be the sweetest kindest person, but if they don't have the competence to reach your qualification they are just the sweet kind person. Don't give them the opportunity to be the sweet kind person that made a mistake and destroyed your life. Don't look at the dog and say," Oh, that's a sweet dog." Look at what the dog can do which is bite you. Protect yourself from incompetent associates rather it's family or friends.

You cannot save everyone. A lot of people don't even want to read this book. You can bring them to the water, but you can't make them drink. They have to have the desire built in them to win already. You can't change a slacker they have to change themselves. When you recruit you're looking for qualified people that can be in your circle not to have to train random people. They should have taken the initiative to have at least started training before you let them into your life. If you observe someone making progress and you can train each other do it, but you can't help a person just because they are a warm body. Be nice to everyone, but don't hang with everyone. Your rhythm may not match theirs go at your own pace. Here is a story. One day a horse is tied to a little donkey by the neck. The horse had to double work by going in circles to wait on the donkey. The donkey in her mind is going fast as she can. It's just that the horse has longer legs and is made for running. One day the rope that tied the donkey and the horse popped and the horse ran 60+ miles per hour. Before he realized it he was kicking up dust and he was so excited that he kept running and never looked back. One lady horse saw him running and said, "Look at that handsome horse!" Then, she started to run alongside of him at or above the same speed. The horse finally met his match. The moral of the story is not that the donkey is bad, but it's just that the horse was made to run. The donkey was holding the horse back and the horse was making the donkey work too hard to keep up. The horse who enjoyed running had to continue to wait on the donkey; stopping him from achieving his full capacity. Finally, when the horse ran at his full capacity and met somebody who was compatible he was able to be more productive. Always find your rhythm and people who are in tune with your vision. If they're not compatible they will deenergize you. Don't drag along unqualified people.

The importance of Human Resources in your life is to invest, nourish, and recruit top people. You must constantly proactively search for likeminded people. The best human potential doesn't just show up at your door step. If you're not proactive in recruiting, firing, and coaching you will allow the just "show up" people into your life. The just "show up" people are people that believe just existing they deserve attention and a better life. They have the mindset to believe if they just show up to class at school they should pass. They may believe that they can hang out just because they showed up in your life. The "show up" people are the type to be good employees, never good employers, or entrepreneurs. They are used to getting pats on the back just for showing up, they are spoiled. They don't see that showing up is only a small percentage of life. It takes more commitment to a mission than to only show up. They have to learn to do above the average expectations of "showing up" and receiving whatever the immediate reward is. For example, let's say we have two students, Student A shows up for class understands the material then puts their head down because they believe since they know the information already there is no need to pay further attention. They come to class excels early on in school because the work is easy to them. They leave school drop their school bags, neglects homework, but shows up to class lectures. The student B they show up for class; ask critical questions, re-reads the material, and solve extra problems. Then, read books outside of class about life. Student A only reads books that the school assigns. The differences between the two types of students is the difference in mentality. Student A believes if they show up for class and comprehends the lesson they have graduated from life. They stop learning. They set the standard of success to a mediocre level. Student B knows there is more to life than what one teacher assigns, so they know that they have to do more than the bare minimum because they have a purpose to learn life. People like student A may work for you one day because all they want is an "A" from class, or a satisfactory performance review from the job by pleasing others. They don't see the whole picture of life and understand that school only prepares good employees. They believe following the assignment or the standard the school set they have graduate from life and knows what they need to know. That's furthest from the truth. Student A types are perfect for following orders. It never dawns on them to use that extra time to learn more and challenge themselves. Don't have "show up" people in your life because they will have you believing showing up and doing your little assignment in a cubby is the way to live. Putting your head down and not observing what's going on around you is reckless behavior. Hang around the student B type who does more than show up. Do things that will challenge you. If student B doesn't become an employer or entrepreneur they will still innovate as an employee by making the workplace, products, and services better. People shouldn't hang with you if they don't challenge you. If you're the student B type of some "show-ups", you would only be the leader of the show-up crew. Most people go to college because it is what everybody else is doing. So, guess who mostly shows up to college; the show-up crew.

One reason why people drop out of college is because they expect to do all their work in the classroom like K-12. In college the student does most of the work outside of class. Class time is shorter and students have more free time which means less structure. Most people can't handle the mindset shift because they're in the habit of just showing up. When they find out just showing up is not going to get it they tend to drop out. Everywhere you go you're going to have people expecting entitlement because they showed up. Because they have certain features, titles, or money they feel they can just show up and receive. The people that say I did my homework or went to work and say they're done for the day are the "show-ups". They believe if they follow a procedure that somebody else made they will receive a reward at the end of the rainbow. They are the ones who gets the mid-life crises because they just showed up to the job, class, wedding and didn't expect to take it to the next level. If people that come into your life can't take you to the next level they shouldn't hang with you. If you've got to keep telling people to show up and show out and all they do is show up you can't change their mind; fire them.

School in the traditional sense has handicapped most people into thinking they can have a successful life because they showed up and did their homework. They go to work on time and do their work assignment so they think they will be successful. They let somebody else pat them on the back and tell them keep showing up and doing their homework and that's it. People sometimes get confused when the school closes when it's summer time because they don't have anybody telling them to show up. They don't have structure, so they falter. The proactive person is constantly moving and working on their next move, so they don't panic when their laid off or school closes. They know what they're going to do because while others were doing the bare minimum they were trying to reach the next level. They know who to recruit and hire to reach their purpose. You have to recruit the talent who believes in the mission. Don't fall for the illusion because you're talented you don't challenge yourself. At the job you get a satisfactory performance review and your satisfied. You get your check and you back again and it's like a circle. Then, it will look like a circus because that employer has you doing tricks running around in circles. People never realize it until it's too late because they were trained from young to follow orders, respect the status quo, and do homework to get a grade. What if you did the test completely right and the teachers still gives you an "F?" What if the employer gives you a substandard performance review and you know it is wrong. What do you do? Ball up and cry? Life is not like school. You must prepare for the unexpected. Life is unpredictable because structure is an illusion. School builds a false sense of structure in people's lives. Being an employee is like school. If you depend on rewards and structure you will be forever at the mercy of circumstances.

You must find your purpose get around you challengers and powerful books. Showing up is not the answer do more. Ask yourself, "What can I do to do better? Your vision and mission may be bigger than what they can see. They may want to work in your organization in life and may be good people or employees, but the CEO don't hang with mediocrity.

If they gain the qualifications to hang with you they're the movers and shakers. People don't appreciate things that come easy. The rewards they get for showing up gets taking for granted after a while because they're only doing it out of habit. Break free from the shackles of the show-uppers. They can't see the vision they may have ambition, but misdirected vision. They are ambitious to show-up. Heck, they might show up early and work late occasionally just so somebody else can pat them on the back. They are comfortable doing extra point assignments that is nothing new to them. Know the difference between the challengers and the employee. They may be useful for your organization, but job placing them is the key. Whatever you do don't hang with the show-up crew. There is no room for show ups at the top; only go-getters.

# Chapter 3

## Live like a Boss

### "I think, therefore, I am" -Rene' Descartes

Mindset is everything. The boss mentality is something you have control over it is not a title an employer gives you.  It helps people to overcome obstacles and achieve their goals. The mindset of a boss is the key. A boss mindset is about leadership. It is about leading your life from the front taking risk. You're the CEO of your life. Your life is your business. How are you going to sell yourself to the world of beautiful people? How will you recruit that significant other to your life, start a business, or get the material things you want? First you have to have the mindset that you deserve it before you will accept it. A lot of people feel they don't deserve more in life. It is all about keeping the mindset that you're the CEO because unless you're 100% behind what you do no one will take you seriously. Once you develop the boss mentality you will have the peace of mind of knowing that you can control your destiny. A boss doesn't let anyone hang around. The boss is doing efficient work and would be insulted if people in their life aren't helping advance to the mission. The CEO sets the vision and the goals. You have to set the tone in your life. The only way to do that is to set realistic goals. A CEO stays true to themselves. Which means they never lie to themselves. They analyze their strengths and weaknesses and evaluate the people in their life constantly. They tell the truth about their weaknesses so that they can develop people around them to compensate for their inadequacies. A CEO is constantly networking. They aren't sitting back and waiting for something to happen. The CEO makes it happen; they take action. You have to take action and get the right people around you. That is when opportunity opens its doors. You may have the key to open that door if you develop this vital mindset.

You have to believe that you can win. If you won and don't believe that you can win you may never realize when you have won. You may not see what you have already. You may overlook your greatest potential. First, you have to know yourself. Then, know the other. The other is anything that is not yourself. You are a CEO. What is your brand? What makes you standout? What do you stand for? You should easily be able to answer these question by defining your core values, principles, and purpose. When you're communicating with people rather that's a significant other or a prisoner. People value your service. It resonates in their memories what you did for them and how you did it. People will share the story of the pizza man who delivered their pizza in a storm. They would share the story about the exceptional customer service rather than share a story from a braggart in a million years. A CEO pays attention to the other making sure he is listening to people and trying to understand from the other person viewpoint. CEO's don't think about themselves all the time to win. People like to be listened to and understood. The best CEO's put the customer's first.

First, you have to know your customer. The purpose in your life will tell you your target audience. Everyone don't fit your brand. Everyone don't want to wear the same shoes you wear or live the same lifestyle. Being a boss is a lifestyle; this not something you try on and put back on the shelf. Once you believe in yourself it becomes who you are and people will treat you like a boss. A boss is a leader. Someone who knows his people enough to lead them. The CEO sets the direction and lets people bring their own creativity to the goals because they don't dictate, but organizes. They lead by feedback from the other. Life is constantly telling the CEO something. In business if you neglect human resource functions like recruiting your business will let all kinds of people in that don't represent your brand. They will come in to tarnish your reputation. Be careful who you let in your company (pun intended).

The boss mentality is your survival tool; your constantly doing maintenance on this tool because you don't want it to go dull. You must constantly sharpen your mind on the sharp rocks of reality. You want to polish your mind and not fear the truth. The truth about yourself and others will keep you grounded. You must accept feedback with grace. Are you a dreamer or a boss who gets the dream done? You have to be willing to lose a battle to win the war. Battles are the little tiny fights inside the overall war. A war can consist of 30+ battles, but it is only one war. The battle may feel important in the moment, but you can sacrifice and lose the battle to win the war. The little petty battles that people try to get you involved in to throw you off your boss mentality don't let it happen. The boss mentality is something you've got to constantly work at. CEO's hang out with other CEO's because they've adopted the mindset. You don't want to risk the chance of anybody poisoning your mindset. Mindset damagers may think like an employee who is scared to take control of their life. The employees want safety, routine, and rewards at the end of the day. A boss's reward is internal. It is knowing they're following their goals, principles, and achieving their purpose. A Chinese proverb says, "The journey is the reward". You have to not only recruit winners, but develop winners. You must inspire people to reach higher levels like you are or fire them from your life. A boss will not lose; they learn. A boss always blames themselves for everything that happens to them in their life. They never blame the others. They don't make excuses why it can't work; they make it happen. They're the thinkers, readers, and challengers. This is the only way to win.

Waiting on a supervisor to raise you above them is the mentality of an employee who will never become a boss. The supervisor will love to keep you as an employee. If it was easy to be a CEO everyone will do it.

**"Tell your haters to take a nap and when they wake up take another one." - Alante' Adams**

They are not going stop your grind. If you lose the boss mentality inside of you, you've lost the game. People in the world need bosses that inspires, sets the tone, and listen to others. People will always be attracted to this behavior. Your life will be filled with valuable people when your Human Resource department is doing its job. The Human Resource department's job is to block unqualified people from slipping in under the radar. The power of controlling your destiny is in your hands or do you want somebody else to take care of you? When you do that you give up your boss mentality rights. When you want the government, people, and money to take care of you, you just sold your boss privileges. It's the mentality that makes you a boss, not money, people, or your employer. A boss mentality is a spirit; you must let it shine through in everything you do. It is your values, principles, and purpose locked away in your heart. You must protect that heart in this world by putting a bulletproof vest on it. That bulletproof vest is your Human

Resources department. If you're not constantly looking to advance your bulletproof armor gets weak because you will be playing defense all the time. It gets worn down because you're not actively recruiting, mentoring, and reaching out. You will only accept "wanna-be's" they come because they like your brand. They think they hang with you just by liking you; they're also called "show ups".

If you hang out with everybody that likes you, you don't value yourself. It isn't wise when after someone gives you compliment, buys you a drink, and you let them join your team without the usual background check. How many spies have been in people's lives? Don't except the appearance of a person. The boss mentality is behavioral, too. You have to act like a boss to be one. Ask yourself, "Is this person a boss or just a very good employee?" There is nothing wrong with being a good employee for them if that's what they want. You treat them nicely, do projects with them, and if they're good people try to challenge them. If they don't rise to the challenge limit your business interaction to only things they are capable of. Everybody don't want to be a boss because they aren't capable of breaking the shackles of having somebody to take care of them. The companies got pensions, checks at the end of a workweek, and sure money until they get fired. The government has social security benefits after a certain age. Until governmental official's vote to increase the retirement age. Nothing is guaranteed. Take care of yourself, your own investments, and everyday try to contribute to the world. Bosses contributes by adding to people's lives, they make things better, they improve the other. They focus on reality to win. They are the practical dreamers who make things happen. Keep this mentality protected from the haters and people who believe in being taking cared of and selling their boss rights.

  The boss job to the employee is to take care of them, with a check, a pat on the back, and a pension. A boss develops his own team of advisors like brokers, agents, and managers. Being the CEO of your life starts from the brain. CEO's are your visionaries. Can you constantly think big to win? Keeping your circle small does not mean pick two people that's it. Keeping your circle small is just reality because not everybody wants the boss mentality. A boss circle practically appears like a small circle. It's the reality of life; less is more. Bosses need time alone to collect their thoughts and to make sure they have their boss mentality together. A boss is not depending on others, but instead chooses whom they want to associate with. A boss must always monitor their thoughts by exercise, meditation, and reading because they guard this mentality with their life to win.

# Chapter 4

## Sell yourself to be Great

**"Make something people want and sell that or be someone people need and sell you." - <u>Ryan Lilly</u>**

If you don't sell you're not moving. You have no flow and no rhythm. The person you are is what you are selling. It is your brand. If you can arouse in someone a desire the sky is the limit; if not you will stay at the bottom. You're the boss and if you can't sell that to people no one will take you seriously. Selling is a natural thing for people not just in the sense of selling products, but ideas. You have to be able to influence the people around you by selling them your point of view. To sell something you have to make them believe in it. Your brand is a promise. Do people believe they will get there promise fulfilled and have satisfactory experiences with you? You have to be able to show people with your actions less words why you will deliver great service. We are all in the service business and selling. Just because you don't have a hot dog stand on the corner of canal street in New Orleans doesn't mean you're not selling every day. People have to persuade their children not to eat candy, but eat their carrots. You're selling to the child your way of thinking on health. You have to show them why they have to give up the sweet candy for the carrots. Of course, you can whip or yell at them to do it, but in the long run if you're not selling something that people understand you're off the mark. You will only create more enemies.

Selling is a finesse it is not forcing people at gun point to do something. These cruel methods of force are for people with no finesse they're the people with no direction. Think about Adolf Hitler who sold millions of Germans to his cruel way of thinking and murdered 6.6 million Jews by force. When you sell yourself one trait should come to mind. When you think "search" you think "Google". When people think of you what do you want them to think? What service do you have to offer people? The sellers of anything must believe in their product. This product you're selling is you. You have to present this product in the best possible light. You want this product to attract plenty attention; so, people are drawn to your business. When you want to be the top in anything rather president of the United States or a local fitness trainer. You have to deliver amazing customer service. That means getting out there and hugging babies or even doing door to door sells. You can't expect people to come to you if you're not marketing and advertising yourself constantly. Television does it all the time in between your shows. Now we have YouTube which is like the new television on demand. There is so many social media platforms now that are making people famous for being themselves. The key to be the #1 seller of yourself is to know your worth.

Are you a Porsche or a Buick? When people think of you in their mind what images pop up? You must guard your brand with your life. This brand can help protect your business which is you. It can protect you from false rumors and the fake people will shy away from you. When people come to you they come correct. When you are a Porsche people don't come to the parking lot unless they got their money, credit, and everything right. They know their place. People know that when they want to play games they need to go down to that used Buick parking lot. You know the product is so good the brand reputation can sell itself by continuously doing what that brand promise. Don't get me wrong you still have to constantly market it. Look at the Coca Cola it is the same drink, but they are constantly doing commercials to keep them fresh in your mind. They are thinking of ways to re-sell themselves. If you don't constantly switch your model or update people will not want to be associated with you anymore because you're not fulfilling that brand promise of innovation. Think about if Apple don't deliver the product people expect. What if one of the iPhones was a dud? People would lose that brand feeling that they have for Apple. Why do you think people love products? It is because of what the brand stands for to them. Your brand can cause people to forgive you easily by given you the benefit of the doubt. For example, when you exemplify exceptional customer service habitually, but make a mistake one-time people will forgive you because they know everyone makes mistakes. When you own up to your mistakes it makes you more valuable. Always take the blame because that is what leaders do. Warren Buffet can go to the bank anytime he wants to take out a loan. It doesn't matter if he owes the banks millions of dollars already because they believe in his brand, his credibility. They know he could get it back to them plus interest. What is your street creditability?

Companies can't no longer afford to treat customers with indifference because social media is holding them accountable. Non-governmental organizations (NGOs) and people will use platforms like social media to protest bad value. When you greet your customers and put them first they show loyalty to your brand. The brand is all they're going to want to wear and associate themselves with. Are you staying true to your brand? For example, an underground artist will make songs for the underground and switch up styles to go mainstream and their fans might say that they are selling out. You must know the difference between selling out and upgrading. Your people should know your brand. If Apple comes out with something new people expect that from Apple, but if you come out brand new do your people accept that? If your fans are saying you're selling out what where you selling? Were you selling, "I am going to stay the same," or "I will upgrade?" Anything that stays the same has no flow; which is a bore. The Apollo Theatre audience of life will boo you off stage. A brand takes a longer time to build, but only a small time to destroy. If people hear that you said you don't like a certain group of people you might lose fans. People need to believe that you have good intentions. If they believe your brand means bad they don't want to associate themselves with that. Your brand must be socially responsible. You treat everyone nicely because they can associate with your brand one day. Are you a Rolex or a fake Rolex? The Rolex company doesn't disrespect people because they're not on their level yet. They still market and advertise to them, but they focus on people who are on their level more. They don't doubt the potential that people can one day wear their product. Be nice to everyone, but just remember everybody can't hang.

If everybody wore a Rolex it wouldn't be valuable. If everybody can hang with you, you would lose your value. Nobody would know the difference between a fake Rolex or the real one. So, stay true to your brand; be careful how you market and advertise yourself. You don't see Beyoncé doing a dog food commercial for all the money in the world. The reason why is because she doesn't want people to think of a dog when they think of her music. She wants people to think "Sexy" when they think of her. Marylyn Monroe killed herself because she was getting too old she couldn't fit her brand anymore she felt out of place. Coca-Cola was made before Pepsi; so, they called their drink "Coca-Cola Classic" to subtly show to the consumers that Pepsi is the upstart. This is all about branding that's why companies are willing to spend millions of dollars for a thirty second ad to separate themselves from the losers. You don't have to get a Doctorate's Degree to create and protect your brand. When you have a brand people can support you as long as you show great customer service. If not, they will tear you down like they did BP when they had the oil spill in the Gulf of Mexico. You've got to listen and show love to your fans, customers, and associates. This is by far your money maker without a brand you're a commodity.

When you have a commodity like soap it doesn't matter which one you get; they're all the same. I hear people say men and women are the same. As if they're commodities that must mean that those men and women have no brand. You can't force people to buy into what your selling they have to see you stand out, so people want to buy into the movement. You have to be the role model for your own personal brand. You don't have to be a role model for everybody, but be the role model for who you are. This will allow you to influence your family and friends for the better. You are selling a lifestyle; a way of life. Your goal should be to make a person feel and look better after purchasing or associating with your brand. You are selling your brand and they will buy everything your brand sells out of loyalty just because you kept it real; think Oprah Winfrey. You have to always be selling. Donald Trump became President built a brand around getting things done. He owns some beautiful buildings and people associate his work with greatness. Hence the slogan "Make America Great Again". Hate it or love it this man knows something about building a brand. You don't want people to have to guess about your brand. You've got to be marketing yourself like your life depends on it. Which it does because you will not eat if nobody knows you exist. You have to dare to stand out. Society teaches you to fit in and become a commodity. If you're a commodity you will be competing with the generic version. Then after a while people can't tell the difference and your out of business. If people can't tell the difference between a Porsche and a Buick they won't see why they're paying more for the Porsche. Then they would just buy the cheapest. Do people know the difference in you? What makes you unique? What is your unique selling ability that you possess? Branding yourself doesn't mean marking yourself like cattle. Your brand is marked by your core values, principles, and purpose and is owned by you. Branding is the foundation that people envision. It is your signal to lead the way. Never do something just for the money that is when you're selling out. If you're somebody that people can count on plus you're nice to all people you can't lose. Don't depend on companies, governments, or specific people. Depend on your brand that is your North Star that people will see and be attracted to. Don't go into the middle where everyone else is be that Porsche. Know that your brand is destined for greatness and people will hope that can rub off on them also. That is why people spend thousands of dollars for that Rolex and the Porsche. Keep polishing your brand and improving it with the changing times to stay relevant.

If you don't stay out and about your brand becomes old like the Oldsmobile that they don't make anymore. Build your brand and don't worry; there will be fake Rolexes, but that just lets you know that you're a trendsetter. That is why television ads make so much because people want to watch the next trend. They are the watchers; you're the doer. Your brand should incorporate giving. People or companies can't win without putting time and energy into the other. You will have to give away things for free. For example, an organization give you free pens, for advertisements. Your brand must have generosity incorporate in it or else it will not survive. The person who hoards all their money shows selfishness. Giving is the new self-interest because it has different rewards every time. Listening to your customers and fans is giving. Paying your full attention to people is giving. The person who is nice to everyone wins. Make sure your brand is known for taking care of its people. The restaurant owner who opens a business, but only wants to cut back on the amount of food per plate will be quickly trashed because people will go to the restaurant owner down the street who gives them an extra piece of bread. People are attracted to people who give value and make their life better. If you want brand loyalty you have to give.

You've got to put time and energy into knowing the other. Protect your brand name by asking yourself, "How can I add value to my spouse, family, and friends?" "How can you make their experience better?" You want to give them that mind blowing experience. If a new brand pops up with the same product your selling, but only gives the bare minimum customer service they will never compete with your brand. People will stay loyal to you for your great customer service. An Oldsmobile can't compete with a Porsche. A luxury brand gives the customer high quality service. How are you giving high quality service to the people in your life? People don't respect a person who is always asking, What's in it for me?" Instead they should be asking, "What's in for the other?" You have to see from the other person viewpoint in order to make sure your brand is being presented properly. Don't leave this to chance people make wrong assumptions all the time.

# Chapter 5

## Television is the Devil

### Television is the Devil; unless you're on it. - Alante' Adams

L et me tell you something; get rid of the TV. It is only a distraction and a time-waster. When you want to win you've got to get out there and do. People spend too much time watching programs until their programmed. The brain must be protected from garbage because garbage in produces garbage out of the brain. If you are constantly fed negativity it is hard to think positively. The television is constantly flooding your brain with bad news and false illusions of reality. No matter what you say the garbage is in the brain and it affects your subconscious mind and how you behave. It is impossible to filter too much garbage in because the subconscious mind is hypersensitive to any vibes rather bad or good. If you feed the subconscious mind with dogma such as, "Buy this product and you will be happier." When program commercials are repeating this message 24/7 your mind is eventually going to say, "I will only be happy if I buy this product." In real life you finally get the product and you're not happy because TV programs are selling you "what you're missing out on" to supposedly make you happy. Then you will be trying to buy another product to give you another high.

The shows that comes on TV is designed to keep you comfortable and take you away from reality. When you're comfortable watching game shows and rooting for the person on them to win it's time to re-evaluate what you want in life. Spending productive hours consuming television instead of marketing your brand is the reason why most people are broke. People are broke because they are being sold all the time they are not doing the selling. Why? Because they are watching 10 hours a day of television. Rich people don't have time for television unless they're on it. Even when they're on it they don't have time to watch the re-runs. Your life must be so packed until where you feel like you're on a show. You're the director of your movie. People want to feel something, so they distract their minds with hours of television during their lives. When they're on their death bed they wonder where all the time went. Television is soaking the living life out of people every day. They are constantly being sold and shown how to live their lives based on actors and actress's scripts.

It is common for any person that watches a movie or go to the theatre to play along with the director's script. We all know it is not real, but we let our imaginations take over. We began to lose ourselves in the script. We do this because we want the movie to take us away. When we let our imaginations take over the brain. It doesn't know the difference between real and fake; this is called deception. Deception is the truth mixed with lies. When the brain loses that difference it is liable to accept anything as reality. When we turn off our brain filter the subconscious mind is vulnerable. You can tell yourself that it wasn't real all day, but the subconscious mind believes it was. The media depicts African Americans as criminals because crime sells. They don't show them in positive roles because it doesn't sell. The African American communities only gets attention in those negative roles. Then add the violent video games and movies you can clearly see the negative role models of the black communities. Protect your mind and be mindful of what you and the children consume. Don't let the television educate you based on whatever it's selling at the moment. Challenge yourself to understand that Television is biased towards making money not telling the truth. Instead of watching television read books that challenges your mind.

Television's job is to entertain you and not for you to think. They want to distract you and make you relax. They want to put your Prefrontal Cortex (PFC) to sleep. When you are relaxing you're most likely not making any major decisions. Your analytical skills are not active. Studies have been showing that people's Prefrontal Cortex activity slows when watching television. The PFC is the decision-making part of the brain. When people are not thinking while watching TV they're vulnerable to buy stuff they don't need and make conclusions about things without thinking. Alcohol can be compared to TV because they both lower the PFC's activity. People do irrational things under the influence of alcohol because they weren't analyzing their decisions. This is the same reason the casinos give away free liquor. They don't want you to think; they prefer for you to taking more risk, without thinking it through. Don't mindlessly watch TV and believe everything on there. Put your safety guard up on your mind and don't watch it. Use your decision maker to build your brand and make you money.

People spend billions on distractions because they don't have a brand. Anybody who watches television for 10 hours a day don't have a brand. You have to be the TV producer for your life and program your schedule with selling your brand, taking risk, and feeling the action. You will become a doer and feel better by contributing to the world. You will learn real life lessons that don't always happily end. The true person lives their life not by copycatting how the rich live their lifestyle. The reason why most people are poor is because they know all the ways how the rich live their lavish lifestyle, but don't know how the rich got rich. Television shows this drama-filled life that people admire because it is being watched. The people who watch wants to be like the stars on TV. Television actors and actresses become role models and people follow their brands. This is why companies pay celebrities to do commercials because people will buy whatever that celebrity is selling. The television watchers wonder how they got rich and can live the lifestyle they are living. The reason the celebrities and TV producers are living lavishly is because the people are giving their hard-earned money away just to watch them.

Instead of meeting the movers and shakers in their personal lives who can get them access to living the amazing life people are giving their time and money away. There is never enough time for Television unless you're selling your brand on it. If you have time to watch television instead of making millions you're a slave to the television. I saw an ad come through the mail and the ad was pricing cable as if it was water. I mean the price people are willing to pay for cable is ridiculous. Do yourself a favor and get rid of the television. I can hear people saying now that, "Television teaches you things." Right, only what they want to teach you to sell to you. It is called educating the customer. In order to sell you something they control the way you think. For example, the "*Are you smarter than a fifth grader?*" show advertisers will want to sell products or services to people who watch the show who are teachers. You're watching the type of shows that the commercial makers want you to watch because they want to sell to you their type of product. It is easier to sell a person a car who is watching a car show versus someone who is reading books to learn how to fix theirs in case it breaks down; so that it can last a lifetime. The television will sell you the new and glamorous. Some people say they can't live without television, they are branded. Television is delivering that mind-blowing experience to them and promising more to come. So, what do people do? They sit and watch people sell their brand to them and they wonder why they are broke.

You are your own television; now go and sell. People want to tell people that watching a little TV every now and then won't hurt. The message they're telling is that negativity and false reality won't hurt. The only reason you should peep at TV is to learn how they are selling their brand; you might learn something. Television is out there in your face; the commercials are louder than the programs to draw your attention. How are you drawing attention? Darryl Zanuck, a movie executive, said in 1946 that television wouldn't sell because nobody can stare at a box that long. He would have been right in the since of their culture and times, but since the television gives people a way out of their unfulfilled lives it is selling. People do not achieve their goals because they're losing productive time watching celebrities. They will buy their products and hope to get rich. Then they will repeat this pattern throughout their lifetime. Albert Einstein said it best, "A person who does the same thing over and over and expect different results is insane." People believe that paying for an advertised exercise machine will change their lives. Until they buy it and it's collecting dust because they're watching more television. They are waiting to be sold something else.

Television don't just destroy you, but your family and the world are affected else well. What if Oprah Winfrey would have been only watching television instead of being on it?  The successful people are the doers. Social media is the new form of television so just because you don't watch television don't mean you're not streaming on Facebook or Snapchat. Time is the only thing you've got if you don't have money cherish your time. Are your sharpening your mind on the sharp rocks of reality or making it dull by mindlessly watching television and eating ice cream?  The television is doing its job of distracting people from their lives to sell them something.

**Television is the only salesman that has their foot in the door at all times. - Alante' Adams**

The African American community is the worst for television consumption. Imagine all that time and money we are losing every second of it because we don't have Barak and Michelle Obama role models because they are stuck in front of a television.

Well what about the news? If the news is important to you; it will get to you. The news tells you everything except how to get money, sell yourself, and how to brand your life. The television shows you the lifestyle of the rich and famous, but don't show you exactly how they make money because then you would do it and it will be harder for them to have their share at the top where there is less people and competition. The reason there is less people at the top is because people are distracted. Television is that eye-candy to the adult that takes the child in them to fairy tale land and their willing to pay a fortune for that. Television is the ultimate seller. You shouldn't hate it because you're supposed to be doing the same thing. Television should be a reminder that you have to be constantly selling and getting your foot in the door. The man or woman that you desire can't see you unless you are around. If you're not seen by them you don't exist. The same goes for that job, business, or brand. In the past you had no chance to compete with television and become rich now you have the social media because people are looking for new distractions. Are you taking this opportunity to sell? Now the televisions are on the phones. How do you like that mobile television on the go? The reason why brick and mortar companies are going out of business is because they are waiting for somebody to show up, but the internet comes right to you. Ask yourself this are you waiting on a television show to come on?

This is the devil and it's probably staring at you right now. Sell it and you're probably on your way to riches because you're learning how to sell. Selling is the human language since the beginning of time. Do you know the language? Don't hide behind your television watching people that are rich and wishing that you were them. Make it happen! People are interested in people you have to make yourself interesting by standing out. Understand that people will pay millions of dollars on entertainment about other people's lives, but have no concern about how they make their money. Television loves taking orders from people who are more interested in other people lives. They will gladly party with the extra money. It is the way it is because people are scared to sell themselves. You can have all the degrees in the world, but if you can't sell yourself you don't eat.

You have to be hungry enough to be a go-getter instead of a go-watcher. If you go into public and stare at man or women without taking action to approach them it would be weird. People would rather stare into other people's lives through a monitor to avoid the risk of the, "What are looking at weirdo?" face. The reason people don't get what they want is because they don't do; they rather watch it. It is no secret; television makes billions of dollars a year on watchers. Television is the influencer rather you wake up to it or not. They get people to change their lives for the better or worse by sending messages to the subconscious mind daily. Don't leave your better or worse up to the television; control your own thoughts. Television is the platform that gets millions of people that are watching the Super Bowl game to buy a Starburst and they weren't even thinking about a Starburst. It is the art of selling at its finest. You call up your significant other when they're not thinking about you to stay relevant, right? The companies are paying TV millions of dollars for a 30 second ad to stay relevant to you. Are you staying relevant?

If you can have the ability to sell your brand through television; why not? The best in the world do it. Are you a watcher or doer? How will your spread your brand by word of mouth, social media, or television? Pick them all if you want, but don't just stand there; do something. Life is moving with or without you. The television will run rather you watch it or not. Will the camera one day follow you? Deep down everyone wants to be on television. They might deny it, but that is why people watch. It is the same reason why people want to be class clowns because of attention. Until the media spreads negativity through their televisions telling them how they can't do this or that because of what they don't have. Do you want television to keep shining on you with their bright lights keeping you awake at night? People wonder why they can't sleep. It is because the eyes are fried by the lights of the television. The effects are still felt after they turn it off. Some people become so addicted that they can't sleep without it being on.

This is the sad reality of the world; we are wasting true brands by having so many duplicates. Find yourself and know about the others in life. Then, maybe the television will find you. Get rid of the television along with people that say, "A little won't hurt; everybody is doing it." Here take this drug because everybody is doing it; little drugs won't hurt, right? Wrong, it is the same song; are you listening? You've got to tune into your own channel and go at your own tune. Some people believe that television don't hurt them; they're in denial. It is like the person that is addicted to drugs saying they can quit anytime. They think they can handle the little high, negativity, and drama. Let me tell you a secret it only gets worst. Don't let negativity sneak into your mind. Don't let the cancer spread. You have to be mindful of your mental real estate. Guard it with your life.

Why deal with it if you don't have to? It's like saying you can live with cancer no prevent it in the first place. Don't fall a victim to the thinking pattern of, "Well, we are only just kissing, and hugging." Next, pregnancy will come. Don't fall for the tired all song. Television and the world will keep singing it to you a hundred times until you believe it and that my friend is the problem. If somebody keeps telling you every day that you're crazy when you wake up eventually you're going to believe it unless you have something that can protect you from the negativity. Guard your mind because garbage in equals garbage out. If I told you television is the best you would believe me until another thought countered my statement and says, "No, it's not because television is the devil." Television do it all the time to the subconscious mind so fast until where it can't guard itself with everything television says by saying, "No, it's not because that's fake or not real."

So, it goes on to believe whatever the television says deep down. If all the people in the world see black people portrayed as being criminals through television the subconscious mind believes all black people are criminals unless people say, "No, it's not because all races commit crimes." Television is war on the mind. Are you a warrior? You must protect your mental real estate.

# Chapter 6

## Money is the Key

**Don't let anybody fool you into believing money isn't everything because people will sell their lifetime to work for it. - Alante' Adams.**

M oney is everything. It is a part of everything we do. You cannot live without it. When you're dependent on the government to give you money without work you're a leech. Once you gain this mindset that money is everything and of ultimate importance in your life you will began to see the hidden power of what you can do. The possibilities are limitless of what you can do with money for your family, friends, and yourself. If you're not in control of your money you can't be in control of your life. You have to take back that remote. You have to program your brain to appreciate the value of money. You have to program your life channel with positive money-getting content. You do that by creating your own culture and brand of getting-money. If you don't have people who can speak the language of money around you, you're on quicksand. It is like the titanic; you will sink.

The music of money has to be constantly played around you so that you can get the rhythm of it. If not you will worship people who have it like people do by watching television. The reason they worship the people with money is because they think the celebrities are gods. They believe they're gods because they think creating wealth is magic. They think they can't accomplish it because the people that are surrounding them in their personal life don't talk about money enough. If they do talk about it they say things like, "Money isn't everything," "Money can't buy happiness," and "I don't need that much money I just want to live comfortable." Review chapter 2 because everybody can't hang. They spread the "live comfortable, don't try hard" mentality. Money is nothing like you think. If you want to make millions surround yourself with billionaire thinkers. You must aim your thoughts on the stars because if you missed the stars you land on the moon. People will sell their lives to a company in return for the illusion of security. This can be the definition of false reality. Real bosses do real things with the understanding that they got to put themselves first to survive.

Putting yourself first to survive is knowing that you have to put your customers and your family first. The companies are not putting you first. Why do you think they have so many labor unions? You're not their priority. It is in their best interest to find somebody cheaper to replace you. The company is concerned about their own business survival, so they pay you enough to keep you barely above comfortable.

If people don't think something is important they don't give it time, right? So why do people work all their lives for money, but have a negative attitude about it? The reason is because they're defeated. They desire money, but is scared to take the risks like a boss to get it. They want happiness without working for it. Money can't buy happiness, but that employer can afford your work to make them happy. If you don't have the mindset that money is everything you will be a slave period. James 1:8 says, "A double minded man is lost in all his ways." If people changed their attitude about money they will change their lives. They will be able to see all the hidden jewels in their own backyard. When you're wasting time at a dead-end job don't wonder where the time went. You're trading your most valuable asset which is time for just enough money to make you comfortable. That is a slave my friend.

The master feeds the slave just enough to stay alive and to work the boss spirit out of them. The boss focuses on the money because they know that money inevitably affects their lives. It is a part of life like breathing. If you let negative philosophies get inside your brain and plant a seed of doubt you're in trouble. Your mental real estate will start to erode. People grow up listening to advice about money from their poor families. The whole community probably was poor. So, the family thought they were telling the truths about money until you they saw somebody that was successful. It blows their minds. The reason the whole community is poor is because everyone likes people who are similar to them. People surround themselves with others of the same background and philosophies.

If the people you're listening to in books and seminars aren't blowing your mind you need to find some new challengers. If you are a business how can you go without money? You have to make the power of money work for you instead of against you. If you stand in front of a moving car you will get run over, but if you understand the benefits of riding inside the actual vehicle cabin the speed at which you will move will be unbelievable. Money is your vehicle. It is a tool that buys you speed and options. Do not stand in the way of money with a negative attitude because you will starve.

Watch what fish do when they are out of water. When you're without money you will squirm just like a fish. This is the reason why people do "get rich quick" crimes because they don't understand money and they are squirming and very desperate. You have to have water to swim. Money can help you move and focusing on money when you're broke will really keep your mind afloat. You have to learn to swim in the money. You can't just ask them in a whisper," Can I get a piece of my cake?" The next person will yell at you and say one thousand reasons why you can't have your cake and eat it too. They are willing and ready to feed you all the negative in the world, but nobodies here to tell you, "Take care of yourself, first." You always will have people telling you that you're the victim to the circumstances and all the ways why something can't work. They are a part of the negativity you must avoid. If everybody in your circle is not saying money is everything with actions you will sink. You've got to have game to get money. If you want that significant other you've got to have game. You have to find your game. Let's say a brother raps to a lady he likes and she gives him a date. He is using game to get what he wanted. If you don't have a game plan to get money you're just a talker.

Talking about money more is a good step in the right direction. Next, you must develop a plan of action to achieve it. Then, act on it. Finally, you'll become a doer. When you're a doer with a plan and the right mentality you're a boss. Bosses don't want nobody to take care of them, but understand they need a team and are constantly looking for that money team. You must have a money team because money is a tool that involves everybody. School teaches you nothing about money, but only how to compete for points and stickers. Jobs teaches you to stay comfortable and gives you pats on the back. If you don't play defense somebody is coming to get your money because that somebody is more focused on it. The best defense is the best offense. So, you don't just save your money and sit on it you invest and have it work for you. The people with the most money knows money is everything. There was a person on television selling a book with the message that claimed, "Money isn't everything" They told people "just to enjoy life." What were they on TV for? To sell their book to make more money. People must wake up. Somebodies always got their eyes on the prize. When you're asleep and your money is in the bank the banks are not letting that money sit. They're putting it to work for them. You must do the same.

Don't live the rest of your life in regret because you're fighting against the power of money instead of learning how to use money for you. People are so ready to drop out of the "money class." They're quick to surrender claiming that it's not for them. They are basically choosing to become a slave to it. They don't want to trade their time to learn about money. Slaves since the beginning of time was able purchase their freedom with enough money. You've got to go and buy your freedom. Freedom is possibility. People go to school to learn to work hard and wait to be rewarded for it. From youth they're taught to compete for scholarships and science projects. School doesn't teach you how to cooperate with a money team to get money. It is a blessing that rich people home school their children to teach them about money. They send their children to private schools or the top schools to build a network. They send them to network to develop a money team. What is the criteria for joining your money team? If you're in a relationship and don't communicate it will not work. If your team or associates don't communicate about money they will not prosper. You have to talk about money at the kitchen table because that is the only way the food got on it.

Poor people are poor because they are ashamed to talk about money. The same reason people becomes slaves is because of fear. They are slaves to their supervisors and that lovely paycheck at the end of the week because they are afraid. They doubt that they will survive, without the job. You have to stand up to that money and say, "I am going to learn about you and you're going to be my friend. I am going to give you attention and take you out and enjoy your experiences" Then, you have to take bold action because money comes to the bold and the decisive decision makers. You don't say, "Can I just get some money," or "Can I get a little money." If you ask for a little you will have to keep coming back for more to live. That is the person who just wants the benefits and no work. It is the person that wants to be a boss, but talks over people and wonder why they don't have friends and business partners. They only want people to pay attention to them.

If you want money you have to have game to get it. Just like you need game to get your significant other. You have to have finesse and not be small minded. People believe certain opportunities is out of their league because they doubt themselves. You think therefore you are. When they believe it is out of their league they're right. If somebody said, "Money isn't everything." I can't waste time trying to convince that person of the opposite opinion.  In their world it is not everything, but their action usually shows otherwise. When life wakes them up it's usually too late. They start to complain about how they can't get a raise because in school they worked harder at getting a grade and they got it. They've got the game all wrong. School gives you the mentality that you can go at it alone. A boss knows that you need to get money with a team of go getters. When people try to sue a company the company has a team of lawyers for their legal protection. When the government tries to capture somebody they have a team of navy seals. When the police go to arrest one person they have a team of cops. They understand that it takes a team of likeminded thinkers and goals. If not they will fail.

The problem stems from all the negative self-talk people tell themselves. Self-talk is the little voice in your head. The negative talk they hear from other people and the television makes it worst. It is like when a child believes in the tooth fairy. They believe it's magic because the teachers at school are telling them that it is real magic. Then they go home and the parents are saying it is real magic. On top of that their little friends are believing it and repeating it too. Everybody in their little worlds are telling them it's real magic. This is the reason they believe in the fairy tale enthusiastically. Hence, this is the same reason why people believe when somebody is rich that it is luck or magic. People think it's magic because their family, friends, and associates are telling them all the reasons why they can't do it subtly or directly. People worship the celebrities because of their perceived magic. The only magic in it is the power of the boss mentality, their team, and money.

Thinking Beyoncé is a "solo-artist" can be deceiving because she has a team of people in her corner. She has to have make-up artists, photographers, producers, road manager, agents, promoters, personal managers, business managers, personal trainers, nutritionists, choreographers, the list goes on. Everybody on her team's ultimate objective is to make her #1. Television doesn't show you the things behind the scenes. This is the cause of the individualistic mentality portrayed on television. It is an illusion. Floyd Mayweather has the money team behind him. So, don't count out the power of money and a team. The only way you can get big money and keep it is because of the boss mentality. Why do people win the lottery and then go broke? It is because they didn't have the boss mentality their mind was only taught how to live with just being comfortable. They weren't prepared for a windfall of money.

You have to be constantly sharpening your mind because that is what's going to make you money because it is the source of your game. You get game by putting time into learning the language of money. You have to rub against money so it can rub off on you. The child comes into the world and doesn't know a lick. Eventually they start their pronunciations after paying careful attention to the adult world around them. If you want to get to know money you've got to get around people, books, and videos that teaches you the language. The fastest way to learn Spanish is to go to the country where everybody is speaking the language. You will learn faster because everybody is speaking a specific language around you all the time. This is the reason the baby learns fast. Therefore, immerse yourself in a money team that talks money unapologetically at least for thirty minutes a day. Practice talking with your spouse and friends more about money. Money comes to the person who studies it. Don't value people who just remember facts that is what the computer is for. The mind is designed to create innovative ways to advance like getting money.

When people were thinking of only horses and buggies the Wright brothers where trying to fly. When people thought they were going to have to write letters to people at long distances Alexander Graham Bell was creating the telephone. You have to think outside the box because that is what a boss who wants to win does. They don't listen to the naysayers that disrespect the power of money they are in the laboratory trying to tap into that sacred power. The Bible touches on the topic with Ecclesiastes 10:13 by saying "Money answers everything." People misquote the Bible and say money is the root of all evil. No, it is the "love" of money that is root of all evil. Remember, a boss loves the people and is nice to everyone that is why they're a boss in the first place. Any person that tells you to walk and not fly because everybody else is walking is giving worst advice than advising you to watch television. You can't change the people who give you negative advice just change the channel take them out of your program. Don't give them any advertising space. You would sell out your boss privileges. You don't have to tolerate the negativity. Life opens its heart to the person who is bold. You will not be able to listen to the talkers because you're busy doing. You can't loss pounds watching television programs like *Dr. Oz* and talking about the show. You have to develop a workout team and do things with people with similar lifestyles. You have to move. Money makes people move some only move to get crumbs other move to eat a steak. Stop fighting over crumbs and get the long green. To get money you must understand the language to communicate with it. You must be obsessed with achieving your financial goals. If nobody around you is talking about money it is because they're not bosses or you're not inspiring discussion. Find yourself a new team or become a better leader.

# Chapter 7

## Be political or die

**"Too bad that all the people who know how to run the country are busy driving taxicabs and cutting hair." -George Burns**

You have to be involved in the world around you. Your network is your net worth. Who they are and what they stand for should determine if you can affiliate with them or not. The politics is the question of how they will divide the money. If you're not around people who got money and who don't speak the language you don't get a share of the pie. This is the information age and if you're not in the know you're out the door. Whenever there are people talking there is politics involved. You can't avoid it. It is what we are and what we do at heart. The mediocre person talks about people, the average person talks about events, but the great person talks about ideas.

If you're not around people that have plans or policies that can contribute to the world you need to find you a new social circle. The person that complains about theory and ideas is a practical person who is carrying out someone's else ideas, but is in denial. If you don't think for yourself somebody will do it for you. If you don't plan somebody will plan for you to fail by giving you negative direction. If you don't guard your mind from people who talk about people all the time your brain will be consumed with what other people are doing. This behavior will throw you off your plan. To be involved you must first know that people is the reason you're alive right now. People gather food, become doctors, and engineers. The reason you're eating foods all over the world at your local Walmart is because the organization of people and labor. This is the way of the world since the Egyptian pyramids. Life is a big pyramid because there is people at the top who have the connections and the pull to get the resources for the few and you have the gossipers at the bottom who talk about and worship celebrities. Are you involved in the politics at the top? Are you talking money? If not most likely you're at the bottom.

The people at the bottom are the scavengers because they only get the leftovers of the rich. If you want to be rich you've got to be connected with rich thinkers. School and jobs teaches you to compete against each other the rich teach teamwork and organization. The only way for you to get something done is to organize. When people get together to talk ideas magic happen. The point is you've got to be linked to make this happen. The only way people can sell themselves is if they have a customer to buy. People do business with other people. When doing business with people there is politics involved that you must be aware of. If you associate your brand with a notorious person how will that effect your money? Politics and money is of very high importance because people operate together. A person who goes to lockdown and solitaire confinement everyday will eventually go crazy. People are hardwired to be social. Don't fight the feeling.

A boss will focus on the economics inside of their social circle. That is all it's about when positive ideas get together they will survive and thrive. Ideas live on forever people die. Politics is social ideas. You can have the best idea for your brand, but if you don't have the money to carry it out your idea gets bought by the people at the top and they get richer. If you don't have a solid money talking group of people with ideas your success is slim. The money talking aspect of the group should push your team to get money and stop making excuses. If you're not talking money that's a negative. People who plan and plot on how to get money all the time will eventually get it. The power of a group of minds together is infinite. Being involved in your community around you is finding the needs and wants of the community. A boss is a leader in the community. They are the survivors. You get what you want when you spread ideas to other people. Things get done. It is not an option you must be in the mix. If not you don't get fed. You get leftover crumbs which means just enough to be comfortable.

The rich lobby the government to set the taxes for the poor just enough so you won't riot. They want you to be comfortable because it leaves more for the bosses at the top. The people at the top hire a team of lawyers to get tax breaks. The bottom is the ugliest because you always have people competing against you for scarce resources. Wake up to the truth and get involved to create jobs to feed your people. I'm not saying you have to be a politician. A politician's career is to socialize to be of service to the people. The person who can raise the most money and be liked the most wins. I'm not saying you have to choose a career in politics, but finding the needs and wants of your community will put you at the top where leaders belong. A boss is a great listener who discovers needs and wants to solve the issue. You have to make sure you get compensated for the good you do in the world. You must get paid for your positive work because most non-profit organizations don't last because it doesn't motivate people to keep putting that extra volunteer time because people need money to live. You have to re-invest in your people by creating jobs and socializing with them. That is politics distributing ideas and connecting people to gather resources to win.

The reason people don't win is because they watch the elections. They don't join the campaign they are the sideliners. People must believe the power of the right people and what they can do for them. You have to be the organizer in the group as the boss. To be political you have to give people your time and attention to win. If you disregard politics in your brand be prepared to starve. You can live in a cave if you want, but you will not be able to reach the top. Remember solitaire confinement. You will be crazy. No one wants to be in a box. So, are you a leader or a follower? If you're not connected you don't have no juice which means your battery is dead; no power. Make sure you're connected to the movers, shakers, and bosses who make things happen. Constantly be recruiting to organize them.

Make sure you stay in business and you've got signal. Can you hear me now? You want to make sure your signal stands out because your brand and what you represent is magnificent. Learn how to speak in front of an audience and you will be and able to contribute to society. All big businesses do is gather talent and use it wisely to make more money to buy influence with people to play the politics to win. Winning is when you're on top because they're the only ones who cares about money and people. Most people don't care, but they talk a good game. Talkers eventually go to the bottom. The bottom always talks down on people. The people at the top is always being nice to everyone that is why they are stars. Your brand must be action behind powerful ideas. Most people just repeat with other people say on television. They don't understand how to be a doer. They would rather watch it and believe it's magic. They will sell their boss privileges just to be entertained which is a distraction from the real moves going down in the world. The magic of being a boss is putting your people first. You have to put time into your community to receive the rewards of a lifetime.

The people will choose their boss because they know you live what you preach. People are your gold. They are the creators. No one can do it alone. So, share ideas and this book with your family and friends. Go to Sambouie.com and get further information on this way of thinking. Develop your groups mind and get challengers to come speak to them. Make sure you pay yourself and your people first when doing business because money is business and business is political. You can't separate the two. You must guard your brand from bad political affiliations. If Nelson Mandela would have not been involved what would have happen to South Africa? If Martin Luther King Jr. would've been selfish what would have happened to the black community and the world? If MLK would have just said, "I have my doctorate's and I'm satisfied with what's going on. I am comfortable." The world would have loss the good that he gave. The world would be different because he didn't organize and stand up for his brand. Now his legacy lives on and people can follow his brand. You have to stand up for the people and you will be a true winner. You should make every member around you better to survive and thrive. The community should be based on sharing and on the principles in this book. Are you a captain that leads people or do you give your money and votes to people that appears magical like the tooth fairy?

Start your own think-tank because non-governmental organizations are reorganizing the inefficient ways the government are handling some problems. The NGO's are pointing out the benefits of the power of organized people taking action. NGO's are holding governments responsible and accountable to the people. You have to be taking action to do your best. Without action you're not in control. So, what is your community problem? You have to go an organize with other people to get the problem solved. One person didn't build the pyramids it takes a team. If you don't have a team you're going to die broke and crazy. Crazy is that person on lockdown in life and don't even know it. They only keep their ideas to themselves instead of organizing to build a legacy. When they die so does the locked away idea. It is your duty to be involved to keep the people fed with opportunity. Don't be a solitaire rat who is lost because they're selfish and self-centered. You have to find people that can take you to the next level and train other people to fill roles to keep the organization and your brand flowing.

What if Harriet Tubman didn't reach back to train other black slaves to escape the cold slavery of the south? She could have easily dusted herself off and blended in up north by not being involved. So, when searching for the right people don't focus on status so much. Pay attention to their principles like sharing, leadership, and intelligence. After building your brand when you're gone people will follow your boss footsteps; now that is a trendsetter. When you have a team of bosses together there is nothing the human mind can't do. So, go out there and mix with the movers, shakers, and givers. You don't have to always give money, but time and energy into the community and your social circle can keep you relevant. When you stay relevant you're on the top of the pyramid. If you take this chapter serious you will find yourself up their make sure you don't forget what Harriet Tubman did. She went back for others because that's what bosses do.

# Chapter 8

## Don't Waste Time

**"Sometimes, the books or people that are intended or designed to remedy my problems may hinder me by waste of time, energy, and effort that often deters productive action"- Alante' Adams**

D on't die with regrets. Time is our most valuable asset. How is it making you money? You have to capitalize on all your time. Get rid of all time wasters like television. If there are people involved it is an opportunity. You've got to understand this because some people can be a time-waster because of the negativity they bring into your life. Social media can help you become rich, but it can have the same vices as television. Perhaps, YouTube and Facebook is the new television with advertisements. You must know the difference between time-wasters and productive activities. Your mission must be to network with likeminded people who have the boss mentality. If you want to use a social dating site, but you keep chatting away on the internet and never meet in person it's a time-waster. It's like the guy who has a conversation with a woman because he wants a date, but doesn't get her number to meet again.

It's a time waster for both parties. Time is what you need to win; so guard it with your life.

How you use your time you're given will determine your success. Everybody has 24 hours in a day be mindful how you divide your time. Your life must be jam packed with boss people. You shouldn't waste a second with any negative ones. Talking with other bosses and positive people is never a time waster unless they have nothing to do with your purpose, core values, and principles. Be open to understanding others and respecting their principles; somebody can always teach you something new. This is the power of using your time wisely. Your supposed to spend time on the people and yourself to win. Spend time wisely because you don't get it back. It takes time to do anything. If you want to become networked and at the top; you need people. You have to be willing to spend money to go out and mix and mingle. You can't be stingy and selfish with your time and money. Remember bosses give; this is what makes them a boss. They give people opportunities by giving jobs and ideas to help others. They pull people up by making time for the people in their lives. How you spend your time determines how far you go in life. Your time and energy is limited; use it with people who can help you achieve your goals. You cannot do it alone. You will waste valuable time because the rich people hire other people and ask for help from their network to save time.

It takes an army to win the war. You will sacrifice your life scrapping because you're scared to ask for help. The rich people ask each other for help all the time. You have to be willing to help others that is what service business is about. Business is about helping someone solve their problems in exchange for money. You can't be a business with no money. People say time is money because you can't separate the two. People at the top have more time because they give other people opportunity to work and help solve problems. The CEO has many people on their team to keep the company rolling. If the CEO was washing windows the company will lose their vision because CEO's sets the tone and if they're busy wasting time washing windows no one will be guiding the vision. You're the CEO of your life you set the tone don't get caught washing windows when you are supposed to be leading the company. If you try to do everything on your own you will go faster, but you won't go far. The rich use other people time and money to make an empire. You have to spend money to get around successful people. The people at the bottom who don't network are the stingiest because they go into relationships asking, "What's in it for me?" You have to be willing to sacrifice some time and money. You do it for your job why not do it for the people you love?

You have to bring something to the table in every relationship. You have to work for others for them to work for you. The boss leads from the front. The boss does more with action than he talks. The boss is also not afraid to talk when they have something to say. Your life relationships with people will determine how far you go. Time is the ultimate equalizer for everybody. We all got to die. You must fill your time with goals to reach and people to meet. You will know if the people or anything is a time waster because it won't help you reach your goal. You must stay connected with the people who are like minded after you reach your goal. This is called the follow-through. People aren't disposable they are an infinite source of ideas and money. People brains are the money. A person falls in love with your brain if they like you for you. So, protect your brain by writing goals of positive action with deadlines.

A fulfilled life is goals with a deadline. If you don't have deadlines on your goals it would have no power to move you. If life didn't end it wouldn't be special. Appreciate the journey by having celebrations and outings with people you love. A celebration is an appreciation of the passage of time. If when the year ends there is no celebration there is no measurement. When you have measurements like a deadline each year it gives the year meaning. When time has passed you will have no regrets by setting goals. You will not be looking for more time because you lived your life to the fullest. People in your life must appreciate your time. You have to celebrate the passage of time with people. If you have a team, but you guys don't celebrate eventually accomplishments wouldn't have any meaning. Once you have no meaning attached to something people lose care; next, their attention. When people don't pay attention that's when problems happen. The passage of time shows your growth. A business should measure themselves over a period of time. If you compare yourself this year versus last year have you made progress? Life is a brisk walk, so be mindful who you take your stroll with. If somebody is negative weed them out fast because that lost time can never be bought back. Your time should be worth more than millions. If you want millions you have to have relationships worth millions? If you have relationships with $60,000 thinkers and you want millions; you are off the mark. If you want a million dollars you have to behave like it. When you're wasting time it is as if you're losing money. If you're the only million or billion-dollar thinker in your group you need new challengers. You need to reevaluate how you spend your time.

$$\frac{\text{Action + Right People + Opportunity}}{\text{Time}} = \text{Success}$$

## -Alante' Adams

To keep people in your life you can't be cheap. Stingy people don't survive and thrive because people will not want to associate with them. People are loyal to people who help them.

If you're the only one in a relationship giving time and money and you're not receiving anything beneficial cut them off, but be nice about it. Money is infinite. The mind is infinite, but time is not. You have to use your limited time nourishing the right minds to become successful. The right people are people with the boss mentality. If you have bosses collaborating on projects something will shake. Jesus Christ saw the benefits of having twelve disciples. You have to be willing to work with others. If you're busy working for yourself, but not reaching out to other people on the same journey you're double working. If you don't ask for help from other people you're double working. You want to work smarter not harder; getting advice from people is a smart move. Who do you think built the bridge you use to go work? People did. You must invest your time into the development of people and ideas with action. Opportunity comes to the group who seeks and collaborate with others. Nobody is born in a vacuum it takes a team of people. Time is ticking down, so you must step up and play hard.

      If you needed to score and the clock is ticking down do you chit-chat or take the shot? People are great because they put time into doing things to reach their purpose. When you're watching people on television they're doing while you watch. When you're staring at the television the greatest in the world are practicing their craft. They are using their biggest gift which is time wisely. How are you using your biggest gift? If you give your time by volunteering for a cause it helps build more like-minded people. America could not be great if everybody had to hunt. Society allows people who want to hunt to hunt. The people who want to go to school go to school. If everybody did the same thing at the same time it would be chaos. We wouldn't grow because people would not have time to work on other important things in society and we will lose out on billions. If nobody specialized in their perspective field first and then collaborated with other people's field life we would be miserable. You can work and try to do it all by yourself, but if somebody else did it for you, you can work on another project which increases your efficiency. You might be good at certain things, but that person may have certain advantages and if you work together you can make a wonderful team. Teamwork can cover more ground with limited time. You can work all your life trying to do it all, but remember time is ticking down. If you want to reach higher achievements and get more work done you must cultivate the right relationships in life. People developing is your lifetime job so develop your skills and you will be at the top.

If people are not at the top they're probably at the bottom worshiping celebrities or talking down at the people at the top. Which side of the fence are you on? How you think determines your altitude. You must have a network. Don't waste your time. Your time is measurement of your goals and dreams. Where do you want to be in 12 years? You have to write down your goals with respect to time and celebrate with the people. If you don't want to deal with people there can be no success. When you open your mind to these concepts you would cherish your precious time to make the most of it. You will start to see the benefits of a boss mentality. Bosses don't waste time with the time wasters they are bosses because they take action. They know their time is expensive so they don't waste it with unproductive activities. Once you spend your time you can't get a refund. Cherish your people with your time; don't just work and ignore people because life is about people. Work and business is about helping people; you can't separate the two.

There is no formula for it; focus on the people and the ideas will be carried. Trust that your people will get work accomplish without you having to watch over them. Don't waste time ever arguing or dealing with petty battles because your losing your millions. Put all your time into your goals and gather people on that mission with you. People follow people who knows where they're going. If you believe in

$$\frac{\textbf{Action + Right People + Opportunity}}{\textbf{Time}} = \textbf{Success}$$

**-Alante' Adams**

this is your formula. The ultimate equalizer is death; all our days are limited. You have to make time for the right people by taking action which helps you achieve your goals. Reading non-fiction relevant books should be how you spend some of that time. Self-development should be your priority because how are you going to help somebody if you aren't straight? Life is an ongoing process each part of the formula can be broken down any into many parts. It takes time, but less time if you've got help. Go to sambouie.com to get more help. Are you constantly looking for that help to get you over the edge? You can help yourself by reading books, attending seminars, and classes. Are you going to spend a life time as a slave or a boss? You have to aim to spend time at the top if you're going to spend time anyway. Time is ticking as you're reading this now. Learning this is a great investment in your life. Time always ticks away unfulfilled when you watch TV. This is taking away value from your life. Put your life in perspective and operate with efficiency with respect to time. People spend time on what they want. Time will tell you what you value. Don't make excuses or procrastinate. How are spending your life?

## Chapter 9

## Respect What You Don't Know And Pay Honor to It

**"If you only know yourself, but not the enemy for every victory you gain you will suffer a defeat" -Sun Tzu.**

You've got to respect the snake. It doesn't mean you have to fear it. You just got to understand that it can bite you and you just respect that fact. Because of that you give it its space. You have to research before you jump. A lot of people jump to conclusions about things they don't know. Don't be this person. The person who doesn't understand something, but repeats what other people are saying about that something without knowing why is lost. You have to know the why behind what you're doing. You must go to the laboratory and do your research. Don't fear it; respect it. If you're trying something new pay honor to it by studying it. Honor is to take specialized study into something. You pay honor to things when you watch and observe. Don't just respect it; pay honor to it. If you don't know a person do your research before you go talk to them because you don't know about them. Don't be arrogant and dive into anything because that is not heroism, but miscalculation. Everything you don't know should be approached with respect and appreciation.

If you don't know something ask somebody. You have to be hungry for information so that you know. You have to study something over a period of time. You don't have to go to college but watch, observe, and listen. That is the only way you can learn which is by example. You must be willing to find role models that you respect and pay honor too by studying them. When people are on the ball they get arrogant and try a new thing without studying it and they lose their rhythm in life. You have to be a lifelong learner. I didn't say what you don't know ignore it or tell yourself it doesn't matter; that's a form of calming your fears. If you don't know about a person really take some time to find out; don't be a repeater of their mere words. You have to be focused on respecting everyone and paying honor to them. In return you will be honored back. It is amazing how many people don't remember other people's names because they can't get out of their head for a second to pay honor to something that special to a person. It is sad that people don't take the time to study things they don't know. It will be a lot you don't know, but when you try to branch into something new read all the literature on it. Then you will become an expert and people will want to respect and pay honor to you in return. Then you put your spin on it. The people at the top are the winners. They pay honor and respect to people that came before them. It is amazing how people see other people that are at the top and don't ask them how they get their money or can they mentor them. They always ignore that fact, but become amazed at their car or house. They get lost in the material world and neglects to study the reason behind how they acquired it.

You have to be willing to get out of your head and do your research on people, places, and things you don't know. School never lets out. It is wrong to say, "Well I'm finished my doctorate's, I know life." That is closing off their mind and they are not honoring the world around them because they want to be stuck in their comfortable bubble. Closed minds don't get fed with new insights. The people who wants comfort always flops because life around them is always changing and popping people's bubbles. They want to hang on to comfortable people, places, and things. They never want to switch by constantly learning and adapting to the changing world. For example, they say things like, "That new generation knows computers better and I don't know nothing about computers." The real bosses will learn about the computer to adapt to the world around them. They are the ones who are taking classes and practicing what they don't know. They are honoring the subject and in return the skills honor them. The person first says things like, "I don't need computers". They first disrespect the subject matter, person or thing. In return they never pay honor to it by studying and learning it.

They never get out of their comfort zone because they are not respecting the situation. If you come into a new field without respecting all the things you don't know you will be in for a rude awakening because you don't even know the basic rules. A lot of people don't take the time to read and learn positive information. When they see a person in a Benz or big house they say things like, "He's lucky," or "It's a rental." They first judge and condemn. They show disrespect to the person. Honor everything that you don't know; if you want something do your research first.

Nobody creates nothing that is brand new. You've got to put your spin on it. There is nothing new under the sun. If you do things without paying respect and honoring the old that came before you're operating in the middle of nowhere. Even the person who is creating something new learn from the past research. You have to learn the history of things you don't know so that you can get a complete view of it. Television shows a snapshot of the subject, person, or thing; you're only seeing part of the story. Research behind the scenes of the cameras and ponder on it. When you pay honor by studying it you ponder on it. You don't just glance at it; you make it your focus. Then, you take action by going to approach that person, subject, or thing. This will prepare you to accomplish your objectives. You must first pay honor to yourself because when you study your strengths and weakness other people pay honor to you. If you don't value yourself you get no respect. How can a person honor a bum? Although most people may not a boss even pays attention to the bum. The boss pays respect and honor out of the principle of learning something from anyone. They can teach a boss what not to become just as much as a person can teach them what to become.

To respect yourself you have to know what makes you different that is all respect is. You have to find what makes a person tick. Honor them by paying attention to them and asking questions and they will love you forever. If you learn about someone else's sport or hobby they will appreciate your effort. If somebody plays golf don't say, "That is the biggest time waster ever," when they invite you out. Show respect by saying, "You know what I never tried that I will do my research." This will make them feel good that you're showing interest in them. Make sure you research what you don't know. The student who comes to class and disrespect the subject matter is disadvantaged. They convince themselves that they were never going to use what they were supposed to be learning. They ask questions like, "Why learn it?" Instead they should be saying, "I don't know this let me use this time I got here to learn because I'm here anyway." People should say I need to learn this person name and what they like to do because I pass this way everyday anyway. Bosses pay attention to the others around them because they are always looking for a boss team. A boss is not a person who don't study life. The people who are at the top is always learning something new because if they don't change they lose and go to the bottom. A lot of people fight because of misinformation. They jump to conclusions and don't see the whole picture. Wars are fought for no reason besides lack of information. They don't calculate before they take action. This is the reason for all the ill-advised wars and mindless deaths. They don't observe. You can't go around misguided because your lack of honor can get you killed. Do not fear it just respect the process that life is a brisk walk and you must be on guard for the unexpected.

Life is uncertain; that is what gives it its spice. If you believe you know everything and don't want to learn anymore you're spiritually dead although your heart is still beating. Whenever your brain stops working the heart will follow. You have to think with your brain not your heart. By researching the things you don't know it will help you years down the line. You've got to invest in your own education. You must design your own curriculum. There is no excuse there are libraries all over the world. People reveal information about who they are all the time. You just must pay attention. People complain that they didn't see the betrayal coming. They didn't see it because they were ignoring that unknown weird behavior. If it's something that don't feel right or is new take a step back and pay honor to it. If a woman asked her man does he notice something different because she changed her hairstyle and he didn't notice she feels underappreciated. She would feel disrespected because he is not paying attention. If you focus only on things that are the same that is when you get blindsided. People will play the victim and say they didn't know they didn't see the warning signs. They didn't see the signs because they ignored them. A lot of people wish they would have gone to school longer and not been so disrespectful to the subject matter. They didn't appreciate it enough to honor and learn it. I am here to tell you it is not too late. You can learn whatever you want. You must go for what you want only after calculated research. The winner of any sport pays honor to role models that came before them that they looked up to. Your research can save your life. You have to cherish this amazing ability to learn.

Research is about understanding and that is the name of the game. You have to find out your game first. Then you learn about the others so they don't play games on you. That will throw you off your game eventually. It pays to pay attention. Don't speed through life; do the speed limit by slowing down. Studying others can save your life. It pays to the do the speed limit because if your disrespectful and don't honor the road conditions life will give you all kinds of tickets. A lot of people change after the event, but sometimes it's too late. An "F" person doesn't learn from their mistakes. A "C" person learns from their mistakes only. An "A+" person learns from other people's mistakes through books, observation, and their own mistakes. The "A+" person respects and honors the game. They don't ever stay the same because their mind is always expanding because of new information. They're the real winners because they are humble. Unlike the arrogant person who skips life lessons because of their pride. The arrogant person are the ones that drink alcohol to forget. They don't study because they are disrespectful to the game. They only care about their name and getting by. They don't see the others around them that they should be helping and giving back to. People can always give something even if it's time and energy. A careless person is someone who lets anybody into their life or hires an employee without doing the usual background check. They aren't principled because they don't take the time to study. They make excuses about how they don't have the time to learn people's names. You have to focus and study the world around you. It takes a real boss who has vision to research and apply what they've learned.

A boss doesn't just passively research but takes action with the information they receive. They understand the cycle. The more they pay honor the more they get in return. That is what the true great business leaders and politicians do. Watching others who did what you want to do is the way to learn; teaching others is the best. You have to teach the people on your team how to honor a lesson. You yourself is game and game should be yourself. A lot of people don't know how to respect others. They want the world only to look at them because they showed up. They are the ones who talk the loudest in the room and are usually the class clown. They are only a tool to be used by others for a laugh, but nobody takes them seriously because nobodies curious to want to learn more about them. They are always seen and people seem to believe they are figured out hence the party's over. You should not be easy to figure out. If people believe they got your game you don't attract attention anymore. The magic will be gone. Real bosses keep people guessing because they're always learning something new. Bosses are always a step ahead of the common person. A common person pays honor to what people tell them to pay honor to. Bosses not only studies the subject the teacher assigns, but they study the teacher as well. The boss looks at the big picture and ask themselves what can I do to do it better? They are constantly trying to improve something by doing research. When a person becomes good at a craft that they practice on TV producers began to observe their track record. The next thing you know their own TV and people believe it is magic.

People like TV because everything on there is dramatized like magic. What people don't see behind the scenes is that the person who's winning is only honoring the game. This principle will never change. The truthful information is hidden between the line. Do you know how to read between the lines? People have to have enough patience to look at the future. You have to research your current environment and catch or set the next wave. Always keep people believing in your magic. Which is work, practice, and discipline. You have to understand that research will get you there and research will keep you there. Don't be afraid to pick up a book. Never disrespect the power of a book.

### Respect what you don't know and pay honor to it. -Alante' Adams

When you have a date you need to study them. Ask them question over time to see if they are a psycho or crazy. Watch their behaviors; you're like a scientist. Be aware of things that you don't know. If you fear it you will give it powers that it doesn't deserve. If man was scared of electricity we wouldn't live as long as we are now. Imagine living without electricity.

You have to be like a rhinoceros and put your head down and keep trucking. One fact about a rhinoceros is that whatever it doesn't recognize it charges at it. When you don't know, something respect it, but take action to learn about it. Don't be afraid to attack your studies and then take action. Your action can be to avoid that person, place, or thing. Or choose to learn it to take it to the next level. Understanding what you didn't know before can make you become a top performer in less time. You don't have to know everything but know a little about everything that you desire. Don't get your snapshot from the television. You have to do more research than the average who get a glimpse of the surface and don't see the whole iceberg. After you understand something take productive action. Get in the habit of researching and taking action. After you're done researching don't fear taking action. After you take action take some more because time is ticking anyway. Did you do your homework? If not you will fail the class of life. So, keep learning and taking action.

# Chapter 10

## If You Chill, You'll Never Be Hot

### Don't just chill with them, build with them. - Alante' Adams

You've got to hit it when the iron is hot. You've got to strike and transform into the shape you want when you're hot. You've got to have fire and desire. You've got to be boiling with passion. If you "chill" you will never be able to truly relax. How can you relax when life is constantly changing? You will be stressed and pulled wherever life takes you. You will not be able to grab life by the horn. You're only waiting to be stabbed by the horns. Life is always happening around you and time waits on no man. What has life will be moving and shaking. Chilling is basically saying, "I'm going to stay comfortable." If you have the mindset to "just chill" that means you're not out of your comfort zone. Chilling will keep you at the bottom. The people who chill in life usually gets cold and stiff. Then life handles stiff people with no remorse. Life is indifferent; it honors the hot and demolishes who's not. Once you get cold nobody passes you the ball anymore because you're out of rhythm. The losers of the world have this "just chilling" mentality while the boss is on the move.

They are focused on their next move all the time. You have to always be moving to get your spirit warmed up. You've got to bring that heat and warm others up too. You've got to be the heater in the winter. When times get tough you've got to be the sunshine and hope to the people.

If you're just chilling your waiting on false reality. If you sit back and sit up too long without your engine running it may be hard to start it up again. You want to keep moving in life. You want to constantly challenge yourself to program your life like a television programmer, but with positive material only. You have to fire the television programmer who puts drama into your life. You have to consistently be nice to people because you want to be the sunshine in the room; not the chiller. You know deep down that everybody can't handle your heat because you know everybody can't hang. You must understand that everybody is not ready to receive the boss mindset. If a place is getting too hot you should already be on the next move. If all the people start to warm up on some information you've got to move into something new. Then, eventually the lame just chillers will show up and make it cold. If the chillers find out about it the scavengers have come to get the remaining. You can be great, but don't put out your flame by chilling. Take action by trying new things to get out of your comfort zone. Move around show yourself that you can be great if you take action with a plan. Business is continuously going and they will sell to you when you're just chilling watching television or waiting on time at a job. You've got to use that dead time for something positive like reading a book, taking a class, or exercising. When you get too cold problems happen because somebody wasn't doing their 'rounds' monitoring to stay warmed up. When you're just chilling you've got to go warmup and get ready. A person who is hot already don't have to go and get ready.

The person who is constantly switching up and learning is already ready. You must stay ready for the ball. In basketball when you don't have the ball you don't just chill on the court and wait until somebody passes you the ball. You must move without the ball. You're constantly looking for ways to do better and create opportunities. The person who gets comfortable enough to chill while challengers are around is sleep. They will wonder how the challengers become so great. They become so great because they are moving and using their gifts and talents. They create their situation because they know inaction like chilling is not the answer. They understand that if they're chilling they are losing. Sitting idle is a crime. People who stay hot will always attract a crowd of people because they stand out. The reason just chillers is telling you to just chill or take it easy is because they are trying to get you to slow down like them. They like miserable people because they don't want to be happy or great. Misery loves company, but nobody likes a chiller not even other chillers.

They are drawn to the magicians in television because they believe that being hot is a magic. They like tell-lie-vision because it "tells lies to their vision." They think they will get rich quick because of their television watching habits. They are scared to warm up their engine by getting out of their comfort zone because they are so used to being cold. They are the ones constantly searching for the distractions like television and gossip because they are looking for something to warm them up. Don't be this person.

They indulge in entertainment they're the ones who is always on social media. They are constantly watching others. They may even hang around you hoping you can warm them up and they can become hot by contact. They will be the fan at the bottom because they want to just chill and watch things happen. It takes movement like action to win. The winners are the movers and the shakers; they're not the just chillers. Anytime in your life where you're comfortable with what you know now; you're becoming cold. When you hang around cold people your thoughts turn negative because it is slowing you down. Your engine may run at a different speed so they are telling you to slow down because they are scared to test their engine and move faster by taking action. They would rather feel comfortable than be successful. They don't want true happiness which comes from being hot and ready for everything. The person that is warming up is always sharpening their mind. They are challenging themselves. They're the people who are making things happen because they know if they aren't they will not be living, but only waiting to die. A person who is chilling will always think of excuses, but a person who is taking action honoring the game finds opportunity and when it presents itself they are ready.

The person who was chilling or planned to chill all day is caught unprepared. They lose their ability to see the opportunity. When you hot people will think you've got magic. When you're always hosting events and can bring something to the table you will always have people wanting to help you. When you're "just chilling" you show up with nothing. When you're the mover you organize and provide. You create more opportunities in the future because you've got experience with situations in the past. You don't just show up to the party you're the host. You have to be a doer. The energy and time the chiller uses to go and get ready when they see opportunity is already being put into the opportunity when it is available by the person who is hot. You have to stay hot by making powerful moves and reaching out for what you desire. If you don't have a want you're "just chilling". A person who is satisfied will get cold. A person who is hot will stay in rhythm because they are always trying to improve and challenge their minds. A person who is hot knows not to stop because they might lock up so they keep grinding for that hidden opportunity. This is why the rich are getting richer. Television makes you comfortable by showing television shows that makes you identify with the poor or middle-class lifestyle. They run shows like *Fresh Prince of Bel-Air*, *The Bill Cosby Show,* and *Martin*. The rich who controls the television wants you to be comfortable. This makes people believe that living as an employee who lives only for the weekend mentality is okay. That is why people downshift and make a complete stop.

They make a stop and get cold because when you're not moving forward you're moving backwards. There is no such thing as maintaining. The maintain mentality is for losers. They believe in a middle. There are no such things as the middle. School teaches people to go to the middle; be warm and don't be too hot. They teach you to fit in not stand out. Watching the maintainers and their illusionary philosophy will show you how people go to work and pay bills just to live in a big house. They are a slave to the house and the lifestyle. They are putting all their time and energy to maintaining their ineffective lifestyle that is why they're not rich. The person who is hot stays hot by progressing higher. When you maintain you're going down because you're not making it better. A person who is going up is willing to even dig ditches as long as they know they've got a plan to be successful instead of the person who gets the fancy job and puts all their money in a house. You've got to see how you can make it better for yourself. You have to fix what you can't see and problems that people don't yet know exist because you're 10 steps ahead. Imagine if Steve Jobs wouldn't have created the Apple products. The reason Adolf Hitler become the dictator of a country that wasn't even his own country is because he was not chilling. He was making moves and he had a plan. He joined the military during World War I and after WWI he organized the plan with his team then he got the money. His plan was to eliminate Jews and takeover Russia and the United States. He wanted world power. During that time it was a lot of poverty and to the citizens who were "just chilling" they thought that he could solve their problems. When you're chilling, and waiting on somebody else to come up with a solution to your problems anything can happen.

You don't follow anybody else's plan unless you check it out on your own first. People who "just chill" are lazy and gives somebody else control of their lives. The chillers are following somebody indirectly or directly. They may not follow Adolf Hitler, but they are wearing the style clothing they got on because everybody else is wearing it. They are wondering why they are not standing out. You can spot a chiller just by how they dress and act. They will dress to fit in and don't join, start, or lead a movement. Knowledge chooses no side; it is neutral. It is indifferent who taps into the potential power. Knowledge turns to power when you use these principles. It can work the same for an Adolf Hitler or a Martin Luther

King Jr. It goes to the person who takes action. Knowledge is only potential power if you don't take action. Chillers will be trying to warm up to the next movement. They are the takers and not the givers. The bosses are the ones who brings the heat to the winter. You have to keep the fire coming by thinking with your brain. Bosses only think of advancement and they retreat only to fight again. They never give up. They are always trucking because they know like Napoleon Hill said, "A quitter never win and a winner never quits." They know if they break through and win they get more fuel to fuel their fire. They get what they want because they are taking action. Don't try to revive a chiller it will only make you cold. When you touch something colder than you, you only get cold. You can't warm them up because they want to chill. Anytime somebody becomes comfortable with the bottom they're in trouble.

The people who are moving are always paying honor by learning and studying something new. They know maintaining, chilling, and cooling is for losers. They're the ones doing things others or not doing; they are the Hussein Bolts of the world. They are at the top because of their sheer tenacity to win. If people lose the will to win and accept defeat they will pride themselves on "just chilling." Then they will lose the world's attention. People think if they lower the bar and get the lower goal that they are okay. Imagine if Rosa Parks would have said, "I will go to the back of the bus because I'm just chilling." You have to stand up and stand out. You have to get out of the cold areas in your life by having faith that you will warm up. You have the potential in you to be great pass your wildest imagination. People believe it's magic, but it only takes time and action with the right group of people. The struggle doesn't affect the person who is hot; only the chillers complain about the struggle. They believe that being rich and successful is a crime; they want to believe it's okay to be comfortable. They watch others do it so they think it's abstract. They don't see that they only have a limited amount of time and are watching their lives away. It would have cost Oprah Winfrey billions of dollars to be watching TV alongside of you instead of on it. She chose to take action and in return she got the hot hand. Developing the boss mentality and shielding your mind from the people who wants you to go backwards is the key. They want you to slow down because you're taking them too fast; it is making them uncomfortable. It takes focus to keep increasing the heat. Are you bringing the heat to the world or are you a "just chiller" watching the champions who are hot? The people on TV are hot hence the chillers at home watching. You've got to make sure you're doing and constantly evaluating yourself for any signs of "just chilling". You've got to be taking care of your business which will keep you hot; waiting on somebody to take care of you is "just chilling".

The person who says I just want to be in the middle class will only try to be lukewarm; it's impossible for them to really bring the heat and eventually they get cold. You've got to be either hot or not. There is no in between so the next time you find somebody saying some "just chilling" stuff know that they're missing out on their calling to be great and don't stick around.

# Chapter 11

## Win

### "Jealous man can't work and a scared man can't win." -Unknown

You have to be so determine to win so bad that you don't fear the consequences of losing. If you fear something instead of just respecting that you don't know it; you're in trouble. If you are scared you're awkward and your rhythm is thrown off. When you keep experiencing something you become less scared of it and more respectful. Then you must become curious and study. It is okay to have an instinctive fear of the unknown, but courage is the ability to trump fear and take calculated action. If you take no risk because you're scared you will get no reward. Life is about risk and reward. When you fear you can't win because you're worried about all the ways you can't win. If you're fearless you can see all the reasons to win. When you're focused on winning you've got to have courage. If you attack the situation with courage and a plan of action with a team who are persistent to win; you have a shot. When you're scared it trickles to your team and your team can sense the vibe; then, in return your team and the world doubts you.

When a person takes action to win regardless of the fear of the present moment winners are born. Think about all your fears like public speaking, approaching your potential spouse, and confronting pressing issues in your life. They are all holding you back from the life you want to live to be a winner. When you understand that your days are numbered you began to believe that time is ticking down rather you're scared or taking action. A surefire way to lose is not to take action. Fear and worry will keep people over thinking and not taking action. It can ruin all the potential of being a boss. That fear turns into worrying about what people think about them. Then it leads to being insecure about their abilities, which leads to failure from the start. The wisdom in conquering fear is to know that it is irrational, sometimes. The things we fear most likely do not happen. When you introduce yourself to most people they are not trying to kill or laugh at you. You can't even fear losing you should only fear not taking action to live the life you want. If you're scared; you can't win. You have to continue to practice on whatever you fear. First, mentally visualize yourself conquering your fears in your head. Then, take action to approach the situation. Winning takes focus and all your energy towards the result of the goal.

Fear is the opposite of focus. Nowadays people fear not being liked on social media. In order to win you've got to put your fears in check by standing up and winning. Being comfortable is an illusion that pacifies your fears. It puts you to sleep that is what your haters should be doing, but not you. You have to stay positive and focused on the mission at hand. If you fear or worry that people don't like you and what people will say you can't win. Sheltering yourself around the TV listening to it tell you that you can be beautiful if you try product "X" is pacifying the fears that keeps you broke. If you believe that you are ugly, broke, and hopeless; guess what, you are. If you fear that something is going to happen it happened in your head. This can cause you not to take action. You have to control the process by visualizing yourself winning and taking your game winning shot. The athletes master this power of positive mental rehearsal and win. People are scared to take action and win because they are scared to lose. Losing is part of the process of winning. You must challenge yourself to improve. If you win everything you don't learn. You have to be willing to gain experience by honoring the situations uniqueness by studying it then taking action. Action is the key to beat out the fear. You must be taking action to win. If you are a hunter and you've got to kill a lion to eat what do you do? Are you going to starve or face your fear of killing a lion? Staying comfortable is destroying your spirit and is eating away at your freedom because time is ticking down. Do not be a slave to fear.

You have to go and take action and come back with a lion. The bigger the risk the bigger the reward. If it wasn't any risk to take action everyone would be rich and quitting their day job. Take on the project you have been procrastinating on. Start the dream you always wanted to start. Do not let fear hold you back. Don't think for one second all the reasons why it can't work; that is fear. How can you predict what is going to happen in the future? Serena Williams can't predict how the tennis ball is going to come back to her unless she first hits the ball over the net and her opponent hits it back. Her opponent may not hit it back; they may miss the ball hence a point for Serena. Do you want to take control of your future? Well take action. You have a way better chance to win by doing rather than sitting back waiting. You have to have the desire to see what's going to happen and learn or win by taking action to see the outcome. If you don't take action you will live with regret and you would never know what you missed out on. What's it going to be taking action or living with regret?

Fear causes many people to mope around with regrets which is only bad past experienced emotions that leads to further inaction. In order to break the spirit of inaction you must take action. The world wants you to win; people need people to be bold because they think it's magic. That is good news for your dream. The gifts you have in this world if you don't let it shine would be lost forever. You are a special gift. How is the best person for that gift scared to use their power? You have to take control of your life by eradicating fear by taking more action. Once you have respected the process by respecting and paying honor to it with specialized study you must take a form of action. Fear is why people lose every time. Winning is not for the faint of heart. If you're scared to sacrifice you can't be successful. When you sacrifice you take a risk that whatever you sacrificed rather that's time and energy you can't get it back. You must believe that it will pay off by achieving your purpose. When you win you are looking at the long-term situation as well the short. To win in life you must outlast all your opponents and challenge yourself to keep going higher and leave a legacy so that others can follow your brand. You have to focus on yourself and monitor and observe others closely. Once you know yourself and know the others you can be a winner.

When I say watch and monitor the others I don't mean be envious. People become envious when someone outshines them and they say things like, " He is not that smart," or "She is lucky because her family has money". Look at the other side of the equation see what the positive things you can add to yourself to become better. Do not disrespect the person by talking negative about them. First, respect what they have accomplished. Then, pay honor to it by close observation. You have to ask yourself, "What can I do to do better to achieve that amount of success and more?" There is two ways you can handle someone outshining you. Watch with admiration, envy, and inaction. Or respect then honor them before taking action to reach their level. You can either hate or love it. When people are busy thinking about the others in a negative light it throws them off their rhythm; it doesn't inspire them to work. It only allows themselves to pat themselves on the back for no work done. When you praise that person positive traits you will be able to see why their strategies works. You may be able to make it work for you if you take action. Don't say you can't or that's not for me. Look at where you want to be most likely somebody have reached that goal. You have to take action and use them as a role model, mentor, or become friends. People are gold only when you praise them; do not criticize and condemn. Winners do not have time to talk about people negatively. They are busy talking to challengers about what they can do to do better.

The challengers are the ones who outshine you and wants to push you to do better. When people doubt or talk down on other people it is because of jealousy. If you speak negative of someone they must be important to you. When you speak of others I challenge you now to only say positive things. If somebody is always talking negative about people change the subject. If they only talk about people you need to find yourself a new social circle. You should seek people that talk about ideas and books. Jealousy keeps you bitter and down; it destroys your spirit and only eats you alive. Do not swallow that poison. Step your game up. You don't want none of that 'magic potion. That magic potion is believing that they have magic and you envy and are stuck in the admiration stage. That magic potion is to think you can't do it, so you call them lucky, or talking about all the advantages they had. You have to get on their level. Admiration stage is when you're just watching. Don't get lost in drooling, but see what you can learn from them. People watch TV to see the magic in the dramatization rather it's showing how easy it is to become rich or a rich family drama. People would rather talk down about people on television rather than take action. Instead they should ask themselves, "How can I get on television and sell myself positively? They are too quick to grab that magic potion of envy. They're the ones who believe in magic so much that they are willing to sit in the front row to be amazed at the TV in their homes. They are gullible because they believe in the magic; they're the person that says everything they try out don't work. They're the person who goes from job to job, relationship to relationship talking about how "the other" didn't work. They should evaluate themselves and not worry about the others so much. You must first know yourself and then seek the others; just do not talk negative it will only make you feel worst.

The television is selling you something so they need you to fill a need for the product or service. So, they flash celebrities in people's face because people believe in the magic. People secretly want to be like the celebrity, so they buy whatever they are selling on the channel in hopes of feeling better. Those commercials know a lot of suckers will believe in the magic. You have to focus on your work and abilities and study others to learn. If you are always talking about people negatively you are only training your brain to see negative in people and in return the people will see negative in you. You respect them and pay honor to them so that they can return the favor. Jealously only breeds unhappiness. When you become negative nobody will like you. Although a person is negative they still watch positive happy ending movies. They deep down like the happiness, but they usually swallow the magic potion of envy. When you pay attention to your future conversation notice who is always talking negative about someone or saying that they" can't" do something. Most likely since their brain is only on the level of talking about people you will be talked about as well. They are the small thinkers who don't believe in the power of ideas. They fear picking up a book because it will let them know that they don't know everything. They are the ones who always got the inside scoop on the gossip. You can't change them change yourself; be their role model. They would probably only see the negative in your role modeling, anyway. The person who is negative, is not successful. You can have money, but if you still feel jealous of the people who have more you're in the same boat. Everyone feels some type of way about people who excel them. You've got to either take action to get better or self-destruct on the magic potion of envy.

Rather you believe it or not people compare themselves with others all the time rather consciously or unconsciously. You have to take control of this process. You have to lock yourself into your grind mode and have tunnel vision to recruit the positive spirited people into your life. Watch and observe the others around you. If you only know yourself you are in trouble. Don't have the mindset of, "I'm just focusing on me." That means you are not paying attention to you because you don't live on this earth alone. You are only you because of the books you've read and the people that help shaped you. If you don't have others that shows you what you're not, in contrast, you won't know what you are. If you lock your mind up on lockdown you become crazy and poor. You've got to enjoy life by not being afraid to talk to other people. People are not good in the sense of the word. Nobody is pure gold. People can be great if you pay attention to what makes them go. You have to pay attention to others because if you go at it alone you will not go far. If you could motivate somebody to take action, your freedom is on the way. After people get hurt by a person they close their spirit and people do the same. The world is like your mirror it reflects to you the same vibes. When you close yourself off from the world rather mentally or physically you are sending negative vibes and in return people don't trust you. If you are scared to trust others you can't do business to win. In order to win you can't be scared to trust others to a certain extent. In order to do business or politic you have to have a basic mutual trust. In order to trust you must take a risk. When you do business it is a risk but with the foundation of trust you can win. If you've got to constantly look over the shoulder of your partner that is time wasted because you could have been doing something else. You're supposed to monitor the others, but not at the cost of being productive. You have to take the risk to trust them to do their jobs, at least, while you do yours.

A marriage or any relationship for that matter can't work if all partners don't agree to trust each other to handle their roles. A lot of businesses or people don't get far because they are scared to trust a person. They are only concerned about what that person can do negatively. When they think like this they're never able to see the benefits and the power of collaboration with a team. They will never understand how to go far in life. The key to going far in life and leaving a legacy is to have a solid team of motivated people around you that you can trust to carry out the mission. If you fear taking the risk of trust people won't trust you. Most people end up poor and crazy by talking about other people negatively to feel important. Inaction breeds all kind of cancers of the mind like unhappiness, conniving, and ungratefulness. You have to stomp out all this by taking risk with people, but the person who learns to take calculated risk with people will be successful. The person who keeps rolling with the punches of life will win. Having a bad experience with a person shouldn't cause people to lose general trust for people. They shouldn't let fear take over. This will cause them to base every decision on fear because they are not able to continue to play in the game of people. You have to take risk in life with people, things, and ideas. You must be vigilant against fear and jealousy. You will not be able to work to win if you're not. If you don't take action you will never have the feeling of winning. People notice winners because they have confidence. When bosses accomplish one goal it gives them momentum to conquer a thousand goals.

The feeling of winning breeds more winning because they're taking action. The people on the sideline not taking action will think it's magic. Winning starts with the mind first by developing the boss mentality. They only associate with other bosses and challengers. A person who is a boss will always be a challenger to the people around them. A boss needs their team to improve because a boss knows that if they let up their people around them will become dead spiritually. No matter what level the bosses are on they know that they must be going higher because that's what got them there and that what's going to keep them going up. It is all about elevation. The boss deals with the mind of the people. If people put drugs into their mind they are clouding their vision. Watch how people take care of their most precious asset which is their brain. If they don't cherish their brain and what they put in it how much more do you think they will cherish yours? People will be more than willing to pump your brain with the venom of negativity if they are negative. Work with boss people and be an example of fearlessness with respect and honor. In the long run if you win with winners who have these principles the victory is forever. It will last in your memory for years.

When you are taking action to be great fear and jealousy can't win in your life. Take action against them by moving in your life. Get out of your comfort zone where envy and fear breeds on the outside squeezing your dreams to a bubble. You will easily get it popped on the sharp rocks of reality. Instead sharpen your mind on the rocks of reality to learn life and give back to sharpen other winners. First write down your goals. Do not just remember them in your head. Don't be scared to see them on paper. I challenge you to make it even bigger than what it is now when you write it. Take action by reading it out loud two times a day. When you wake up and when you go to sleep. You need to put a deadline on it and write what you will sacrifice to reach it. Carry it with you everywhere. Remember nothing comes without a risk; take the shot. Your goal must be specific as possible because the more you can focus the mind in the specifics the better it's able to plan appropriately. Take action; don't take to being scared. Jealousy is for the loser; join the winners circle.

## Chapter 12

### Pleasure is Lethal

### "Suffer the pain of discipline or suffer the pain of regret" -Jim Rohn

There is a price you pay chasing pleasure. Pleasures in excessive amounts can blind you to unfortunate consequences. It can cause massive setbacks and unnecessary failures in life. Pleasure causes some people to go blind to the position around them. They are so willing to dive into the situation until they ignore the warning signs. The pleasure usually has strings attached. There is a price you pay for blindly only seeking pleasure. There is a saying that says, "No pain, no gain." If you're only taking action for excitement seeking things you are off the mark. People get married just for the pleasure side. Once in they don't enjoy the work side. Anything in life that you want takes work. Rather it's other people's work, but nonetheless work must be performed. This culture shows a lavish lifestyle of celebration for the rich and famous and people notice this and want to imitate the play side. You must be aware that you not only imitate their play side, but observe the business side as well.

A lot of people have babies because of pleasure. The sex act alone is pure pleasure and as an affect a baby comes along. The cost of pleasure is steep you must moderate your pleasure. When you love your friends that is pleasurable. Going into business with your friends can be lethal because you're not focused on the bottom line only pleasure. When the pleasure stops and the pain comes in nobody knows how their friends will react. Everyone wants to party, but no one wants to bake the cake. The person that enjoys and is passionate about taking care of business will have an advantage. The person who loves to bake the cake which is the work side of the business will be great. When you make life decisions based off pleasure you are at a disadvantage. It takes pain to practice and read non-fiction books for hours. Reading the relevant books takes pain; reading irrelevant books for pleasure is superficial. It takes a little pain to take action consistently. A lot of people are naturally seeking the fast pleasure. They want the opposite sex, money, and respect fast. Anything in life that is worth something you must grow to get it. It requires for you to move out of your comfort zone. It puts you in that pain zone to grow.

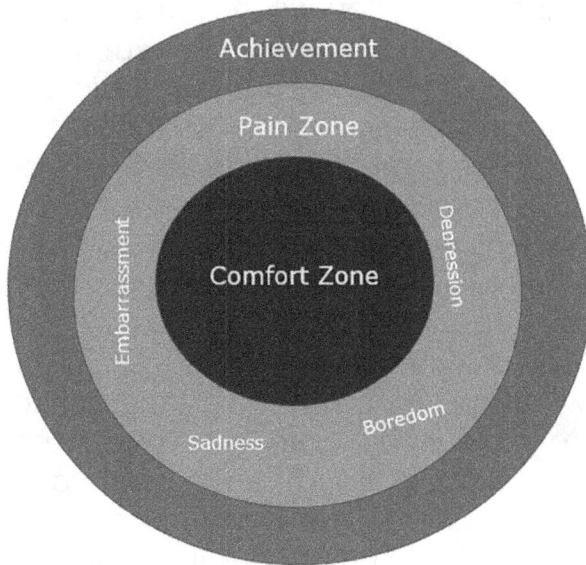

When your only motivation is pleasure you are like a cat and somebody else is pulling the yarn. The cat will just keep following that yarn distracted by pleasure. This can cause the cat to run into traps. People like that have no finesse and somebody will see them wearing their pleasure on their sleeves. You should want the everlasting pleasure of knowing that you stayed true to your core values, principles, and purpose. The everlasting pleasure is to win at reaching your personal dream without quitting. If you have a goal of where you want to be in life you must avoid the eye candy. The eye candy pleasure will look like an eye sore to you when you become discipline minded. You will become less distracted against instant gratification. Everything in our culture is saying you need it fast, quick, and now. You must avoid this illusion. McDonald's do not feel you up, but you can get it fast. McDonald's can't do both feel you up and get it to you fast. It takes a while for steak to cook. It takes time to build an empire. When you seek pleasure with television, gossip, and events instead of sticking to the bottom line you will be a loser. You have to stay aware of the poison ivy on the outside of the pleasure. Before you grab at it you better know what you're doing. You have to train your mind on the big picture to get that delayed gratification. Just because your car goes 180 MPH doesn't mean you should go 180 MPH because you know the consequences could be deadly. You must drive safe to get to the destination. Engineers and scientists have planned the safe speed backed up by the law. When you set out on your course in life plan it like the engineers and then drive safely. Back up your safe driving with your principles. Nobody's going to tell you to slow down on the pleasure, but life will give you tickets.

You must put out the fire of immediate pleasure with better discipline. The immediate discipline will keep you focused for the long run. In the short and long run discipline is your best friend. Your motivation should be internal. Your motivation shouldn't be for exterior rewards and pats on the back. That is the employee mindset.

The employee seeks the pleasure of the traditional pat on the back. You're a boss that celebrates with your team, but that is not what drives you. You must be careful what you associate in your mind with pleasure. The effects of pleasure can pull you away from your long-term goals. The person that says, "Let me just try it this one time." That just this one time can alter their life by getting them hooked. You've got to monitor your weakness for immediate pleasure. Your ultimate pleasure to fulfill your purpose is a spiritual battle. You cannot let the physical pleasure outweigh your spiritual pleasure. Your spiritual pleasure gives you the energy to reach your goals it helps guide your discipline.

Seeking pleasure is when you are out of control. The pleasure of sex and money is great. It becomes a problem when all you see in money and sex is the pleasure it can bring, but not the amount of responsibilities that it entails. You want to see both sides of the equation when it comes to pleasure. Sex and money has its price. You must put the pain of discipline in to get the pleasure. If you believe in pleasure, but no discipline your money will part. A fool and his money will surely part. When you are making money you must be disciplined enough to reach back and give to others your time, some money, and energy. When you have this weakness for pleasure to go 180 miles per hour you must have the discipline to drive slower so you can watch for pedestrians; which are the others. You've got to constantly be the defensive driver on your course of life by watching for potholes and other people. When you are a pretty woman or handsome man don't indulge in the attention. Work on getting better at a skill so that you can have beauty and brains. Run away from the pleasure of attention if it becomes a distraction. You do not want to become a frozen deer in the spotlight. When you become unproductive and distracted take a step back. Do not panic when you fall short of your goals. Pay attention to the others don't let the bright light of attention blind you. The reason people fail in life is because they forget about that other. The wisdom from slowing down and watching and honoring that other is the key. It is easy to seek pleasure and try to avoid pain. People want to seek pleasure, but they run from pain which is discipline. Pain will find them because life without pain gives you no reason to seek pleasure.

If you focus on disciplining your mind for the long shot ten, twenty, and thirty years down the line you will have the real pleasure of reaching a meaningful goal. If you seek security because it's pleasurable you will never be great. The greats understand that security is an illusion. Our time is limited even our children are not secure no matter how much money you've got. Your children and everyone else on this earth must have discipline. You've got to have the fire and desire that makes you disciplined enough to get the everlasting pleasure of staying true to yourself. This spiritual feeling will empower your mind and energize you to attack your problems. The reason other people stay at the bottom is because they have the "Hakuna Matata" mentality. It is causing them their life; they better wake up. Relationships of all sizes entails the pain of work such as checking on them. You have to listen to them and work together as a team. This is what bosses do. They don't just hire people into their life without monitoring them. You have to continuously pay attention. Don't get sucked into the pleasure where you stop paying attention because pain will find you.

In life you must seek that necessary pain to gain. You've got to have the discipline into your program. You must develop a program to get you where you're trying to go. When you develop your program you must do the dirty work it requires for you to make it run. Life is about the trenches because it is a spiritual war. The spirits of procrastination, inaction, and immediate pleasure are taking the things you desire away from you. You should feel relieved to attack pain because you know it's going to pay off. You should take pleasure in constantly being in the trenches of life. In the trenches there is mud soaked boots, bullets of envy, and fake people whistling pass your head. You must have the discipline to stay down and focused in the trenches to win the war. You want to be the last one standing when the dust settle. A lot of people want to look up and say, "Look at me." Others at the top are like a rhinoceros they're putting their heads down and are continuing to truck. You must have the discipline to stay focused on the goals you want. Anytime you let your guard down to the venom of instant pleasure you are facing a setback. If you're an ethical business person that allows sex and bribery to tempt you your spirit is down. When you take the potion you feel regret. Life is too short to take all kinds of distractions. You must protect your mind from the pleasure of now to win the war later.

A lot of people say things like, "Man, if I was young again." You may also hear talks about the good ole' days. The people in the trenches always believe the good ole' days are ahead because they train every day. They don't stop working out because their weight isn't what they expect or because they are too old or too young. They're not concerned with keeping score when they're working out because they work out regardless of their weight. They know they're working out to increase their self-esteem and improve their overall health. They don't stop and start because they are focused only on their external weight. They are motivated because they believe in the principle of staying in the trenches. They know deep down that the people who believe in the magic potion of stepping out of the trenches one day is disillusioned. When you have the money and success that's when you should really be in the trenches because you are a bigger target. The people who work out for their health stays in the gym for life. They don't stop every second and ask, "Are we there yet? They are the ones who finish what they started because it's in them spiritually not on them.

They put their heads down and truck because they know it's the reason they keep moving. When you move you keep the body and spirit in motion. You don't stop moving because somebody's not paying you. You keep going that's how you're going to keep your spirit up; that's what's going to make you a winner. Do you do maintenance on your tools? Your tools are your internal will to win. Sometimes you've got to check yourself. You want to know if you're in it for the health. The pain of a workout will eventually turn into enjoying that soreness because you know that soreness is only a sign of progress. You're not going to look at the grind like it's a liability. You are going to stay looking at it as your only asset because your time and grind is all you've got. You've got to work. Bill gates don't have to work but the same spirit that made him a billionaire is still in him that is why he works today. Some people say they can't wait to retire. Retirement is a manmade concept that basically says you don't have to work at a company because you saved some money. It doesn't mean don't work because that is not a winner. Donald Trump is a billionaire and he works. Oprah Winfrey is a billionaire and she works. If you believe that just because you don't have to work means you should not want to work.

Keep reading this book until you are to the point that you desire the trenches.

The trenches are your headquarters while everyone else is running from the battles of life. You are in the trenches taking action and planning. This is where you are at your best. This is what makes you bold and give you the charge to win. Understand it takes necessary pain to grow in any endeavor. If it is your goal to be true the trenches is your truth. The trenches are where you do your homework for life's classes. The trenches are where you give or volunteer for places when you would rather want to watch TV. The trenches are where you may have to leave people behind because they don't want to grow. The trenches are where you get a piece of reality to sharpen your mind. You have to embrace the trenches because it's the only thing that's keeping you real. Real diamonds only sharpen real diamonds. If you are chasing pleasures you are not in the trenches. You become an easy target. People don't reach the top because they are mostly likely reckless. If you don't control your immediate pleasures you will never have a peace of mind because you will have no control over your destiny. You will be like a child who eats all the candy, but as an adult has no healthy teeth. Your personal guardian is your program of discipline. To win the war you must have a personal program with a strategy behind it.

When you go to school the program is to teach you to be an employee. When you watch television they teach you to watch. As a matter of fact they don't want you to move because they are making it happen by using your time, money and energy. TV is very disciplined because they're relentless and persistent in the trenches. The people on there be working on the next show while you are watching the last. You must have that relentless discipline to advertise and promote yourself like television. What is your rating? Are people tuning in? When all the citizens of Rome are in the Roman Coliseum Rome will be falling because people are not protecting the borders. They're not doing their 'rounds' to watch for the enemy. They're not trying to make Rome better. They began to love pleasure so much that they forget to monitor and pay attention to their surroundings. They are so busy watching the gladiators battle it out until where they don't know what's going on around them. They are so busy watching modern day *SportsCenter* that they lose themselves in the pleasure. This pleasure will be the cost of collapse. Meanwhile, when you are in front of your pleasure there is an entrepreneur in the trenches somewhere holding down that job for you. After people have their pleasure for the weekend they go and give their time, energy, and effort to the job the entrepreneur provides all week. The goal should be freedom out of that serfdom. People go to work to pay rent and then chase the pleasures of what the weekend got to offer. This pleasure cycle will get you washed up. When you are washed up your spirit is low. When you have a low spirit you are a ripe to be a slave.

It is only the trenches if it makes you stronger. When you try again and apply what you learned last time you will get the benefits. When you force yourself to have discipline you force yourself to be a winner. The trenches are your friend against distracting pleasures which is your enemy. The trenches get tougher and more challenging; it keeps you growing stronger. Anything that comes fast is a lie. Don't buy lottery tickets because it is promoting the wrong spiritual vibe. It is the spirit of waiting for something to happen. It is waiting for somebody to give you something like a load of money. This mentality causes you to wait and watch. Drop the mindset that thinks it's only two dollars because that's what the government wants you to you to think; along with everyone else. That is why the lottery is worth millions of dollars because everyone is saying, "It's only two dollars." Stop participating in those little pleasures and tricking yourself into believing that TV commercials are going to help you lose weight if you pop a pill. You don't want anything fast because it comes with side effects. If you take a pill the side effects are going to be death; blindness, heart stroke, you name it. The television comes into your comfort zone to sell you a lie or a dream. It is like a hunter when it is not hunting season to come into a bear cave while their hibernating and kill bears. They know you're watching TV because your bored, weak, and vulnerable so they manipulate your minds by saying, "Hey, you don't have to get out of your comfort zone just swallow this because you are already eating ice cream and watching TV anyway."

You have to embrace boredom as discipline. Everything you do is not going to be fun. I bet doing 10, 000 lay ups over and over isn't fun for Michael Jordan, but the game keeps him improving for the long run. What could be worst accepting boredom or wasting your life away. Go and get your significant other, that job you want, and that body you desire. Don't do it just for those reasons, but go into the trenches for yourself because you know in the long run it will pay off. Anything that is fast is reckless! Do not do anything rushed that includes marriages, jobs, or swallowing pills. You must weigh them out because only time will tell. You don't know your own self in two years, how do you think you will know about others in two years? The rule of thumb for marriage is to wait ten years dating before you sign the paperwork. When you marry because of the pleasure of "love" or without a prenup you can ruin your life. When you have children it takes a quarter of a million dollars to raise them until they turn 18; not including college. If you don't have the money it can ruin the children's lives and yours. You must have your money right when you marry. The pleasures of children and marriage cost, and not just in dollars and cents. 50% of marriages end in divorce. If you want to be at the top don't believe the lies that you're 100% different and that you can save someone and change them.

People must help themselves by learning discipline. If you take pleasure in helping people, that same person, on the flip side can take pleasure in taking advantage of people that helps them. You have to monitor people and watch your pleasure. You should think with your brain and not your heart. Do not get into a partnership like marriage if you've got to constantly "fix" them. A partner should already work you shouldn't have to fix them, but do your maintenance by monitoring them and challenging each other. A partnership should work because you guys should be moving in the right direction and have shared core values and a vision. The pleasure of being at the top should not be associated with living to keep up with the Joneses. Practicing discipline should propel you to the top regardless of the circumstances. Your positive spirit will make you a leader regardless of the external circumstances. To be rich spiritually you must first know the spirit of the trenches. When you have the desire to leave the pain of the trenches that is when your mind becomes dull and you lose your Midas Touch.

# Conclusion

## "Winning is something, but participation is everything" -Debasish Mridha

The game itself is the reward.  To be able to play is the pleasure. There is no pleasure in not playing because being on the sideline watching others is not useful. People should not be on the sideline envying others bickering or complaining. It's about action. When you tap into the power within you, you become a dominating force in the game. The feeling of importance you get for taking action and not being on the sidelines like useless product is energizing in itself. Most people are sideline players. Although, they have the desire to be in the game they would rather complain and whine and doubt people who play the game. The reason is because they don't have the confidence or the will to embrace the pain of the game or they aren't willing to sit down and learn to observe the players. They want the real players to feel like useless product like they do. They chase the illusion of external rewards like immediate attention and bluffing to feel like a real player. A player must be humble and don't have time for postulating because they're putting in the time by taking action.

Real bosses are getting rewarded by feeling alive because they are a part of the process.

When they manage to deal with the up's and down it gives them confidence that others don't have. That confidence they develop is critical to the boss mentality. Some people will hate the boss because they have the confidence in them that they don't have. A true boss can't hang with the sideline "wanna-be" bosses because they can't understand the practical insights of a true boss. The sideline players are hiding behind theories and abstract concepts that makes them feel secure about being comfortable. They believe in their own lies because it comforts them. They don't want to ask themselves the tough practical questions because they are insecure. The real bosses accept the sideliners as a part of the game. A boss knows that they want to take his spot deep down. A "wanna-be" boss don't believe they deserve it and they're comfortable being on the sideline. They don't want to leave their comfort zone until they get cut in life by a loss of a job or the boss. They find any excuse to justify their believe system of why they are being a loser. The "wanna-be" bosses enjoys when a boss tries and fails. The viewing of a boss failing only makes them feel all the better because it justifies why they shouldn't take action. They want to pull you down to their level so you won't challenge them. A boss will see through their half thought out ideas and lousy ideas because they're ten moves ahead of them and constantly learning and perfecting their craft which is the ultimate feeling of pleasure.

The skills to deal with the practical puts the boss ahead of a theorist who doesn't take action. The boss is building confidence and is not fazed by the doubters. The feeling of a boss mastering the game will motivate them to do more. A boss knows the sideline is a spiritual death and avoids people who are on the sidelines. They don't negotiate with them or preach to them using words to rouse them up. They know they won't listen anyway because they don't respect and honor the game. A boss loves solitude to collect his thoughts. A boss knows some people will be envious and wants to be like him. A boss accepts the realities of being a boss because that's the only thing practical to achieve. With a boss mentality you can't lose because the act of losing is being on the sideline. Winning is being a boss regardless of the external reward. The external reward is illusionary and is more of hindrance because it can blind you and you may loss the flow of the game. When you lose your flow you suffer because you were focused on the reward or toys. A boss only under certain conditions accepts a qualified reward. It must meet certain conditions before they receive it. A boss pride themselves even on the type of rewards they accept. They play the game knowing the ultimate reward is the feeling that they played and don't have to ask for more playing time at their death bed. The reason is because they know they did their best. For example, if sex, money, and success comes at the cost of breaking their

~ 137 ~

principles they will not accept the so-called reward. Everybody wants to hang with a boss because they think it's going to rub off on them. This boss mentality must be studied daily and practiced.

A boss will avoid the false rewards which will only make people respect them more because a boss will never go out their way to chase nothing: sex, money, people or things. Man will honor the truth with respect which is what the boss plays for and never the limitations of external rewards. They appreciate the acquired taste in the aesthetic concept of the intangible feelings of respect. They get respect because they are respecting themselves by keeping the boss mentality. People come and go, clothes come and go, but the boss mentality is forever. Respect it and pay honor to it or move to the sidelines meaning get out the way. A boss pride themselves by learning, taking action, and focusing on the details of the game. In return the worries of the future dissolves and they have more rewards than they'll have time for. A boss always raises their options because they expect more and life gives it to them because they earned it. When you are honoring the rules you can die a peaceful death and rest knowing you never hung with side liners.

What would you do when you join a group of likeminded bosses in a supportive environment where you can collaborate with other bosses that will help you keep your mindset sharp and hold you accountable that allows you to stay on track so that you can be successful?

"An environment that stimulates you to soar by motivating you with a proven structure that is committed to your personal success. Where you can get targeted advice from other bosses within minutes."

How satisfying would it feel to be able to be a part of an exclusive group of people who has the boss mentality that accepts and understands you?

You can have this simply by joining a Master Mind Group. A Master Mind Group is a term coined by Napoleon Hill author of "Think and Grow Rich." Which is "The coordination of knowledge and effort of two-or more people who work toward a *definite purpose* in the spirit of harmony. No two minds ever come together without thereby creating a third, invisible intangible force which may be likened to a third mind." Hence the term 'mastermind'.

Because as everyone know we are limited to our geographic area you couldn't connect with people before the internet with like minds automatically because it would be too time-consuming to find them in the various locations they live by random chance. You can go through years just trying to find them. Then, you have to make sure you guys are on the same page. Then, you have to make time to meet up with them consistently.

Finally, you will not really know what their mindset is unless you know what kind of books that their mind processes. How can you find that out? You can do it by tediously interviewing everyone you meet but that can be intrusive. Then if they just so happened to read a book or two that is proven it doesn't mean they are getting something out of it unless you discussed those books with them personally to verify for yourself.

You don't have to go down that road now that you understand the importance of time-management, core values, principles, purpose and having a vision. You are now prepared to see the value in likeminded individuals plus with the power of the internet you are not limited to your geographic area anymore. You don't have to leave your mind vulnerable to random people and be a slave to random chance and geographic limitations anymore. You can easily connect with like mind people in Sambouie's Master Mind Group at will wherever you are at any time without costly recruiting. I wonder how quickly *you are going to join Sambouie's Master Mind Group.* It will be like your own personal board of directors. Plus, they will challenge you when you need a kick-start by having riveting discussion of innovative concepts that enhance your creative thinking. Simply login and bam! This will allow you to do more in less time in a supportive environment to reach your full potential.

Imagine having a team of people rooting for you to win. A team of likeminded innovative people who care about your success and is willing to automatically contribute to helping you out.

Sambouie's Master Mind Group isn't just any randomized group. Unlike most other groups Sambouie's Master Mind Group fosters discussion of **proven books**. Which has evidently been found to be the best way to retain knowledge according solid research. When you discuss concepts with other people you tend to remember more of the crucial concepts which means the more you can apply it in your life without wasting time alone reading random unproven books in your corner of the world.

When you increase your knowledge it leads to better understanding which alters your actions for the better which leads to next generation results. By simply being careful what you put into your mind you will be half way to reaching success. As you know all science communities know that peer-review of research is key to determining if the concepts are credible and reliable.

Clearly, we know we can't jump to do every activity because we know we have limited time. So, the wise way is to prioritize specific activities that will help propel you to your purpose. By learning from others with experience and books you save yourself from wasted time, energy, and effort.

When you have a team of others readily researching and studying with you based on the principles of this book you increase your power because you will have others researching which gives you feedback and perspectives from different angles.

This will give you the ability to make better informed decisions because you will see the big picture and never get side-tracked. *The more you understand the power of a Mastermind group the more you'll realize you need to join Sambouie's Mastermind Group.* Having a mastermind group is like full-coverage insurance for your success. The focus on researching, studying, and growth will help keep you grounded in the key aspects of life to be successful because you have a solid team to see you through that focuses on the essentials you need. The more you read the more you won't want to be without a Mastermind Group. When you are not at your best your teammates will support you and when you teach others it is the best way to learn because it helps make the message a part of you. Which will help you become a better noble leader. This unique design of the Mastermind group guarantees exponential improvements in your business and personal life. Sambouie's mastermind group focuses on your essential needs first to prepare you for your success.

*This is not a class* this is a self-development program design to electrify your path to success with all the right web of people and proven environment you need to spark your growth.

As you *act on my advice* and join the Sambouie's Mastermind group right now. You will enhance your life because you will have the help you need to get the time freedom you want and get value everyday forever.

Here is some of the benefits you will get when you join Sambouie's mastermind group.

- It gives you the structure needed to encourage and motivate you to continue to grow and avoid pitfalls.

- It is like having an interactive support team that will offer you the help when you need to overcome your circumstances to achieve your goals.

- This will be a marvelous group that gives you solid recommendations and generates creative ideas based on powerful discussions.

- Allows you the best methods to discover answers to specific questions that are troubling you while getting targeted advice to help solve your problems so that you can achieve more success.

- It will be a fertile environment that fosters you with the essential tools you need to get more done with less.

While you are sitting here wrapping up this book you begin to understand why you can't afford not to join Sambouie's Master Mind Group. This group will be made up of people who relate to you and will be in rhythm and harmony with you. This will allow you to communicate more effectively to get more done because they will understand you. The design of the program is used to encourage your self-development which is the best role that you can acquire on your journey to success. Plus, it is built on discussing ideas and strategic implementation which is proven to be the best way to learn.

*Now that you've read "You May Already Have What It Takes – The Art of Winning." I'm sure you realize that you must join Sambouie's Mastermind Group now so that you can secure your mind from negativity and enhance your business and personal life.*

Hurry sign up for Sambouie's Mastermind group now by going to Sambouie.com and register in the Master Mind Group to follow-through with likeminded people to execute your plans with success.

## Contact the Author

**Email**:

sambouie@sambouie.com

**Website**:

Sambouie.com

Sambouie.tv

**Facebook**: @Sambouie

**Instagram**: @alanteadams

**Youtube.com**: @Alante' Adams

www.ingramcontent.com/pod-product-compliance
Lightning Source LLC
Chambersburg PA
CBHW061745270326
41928CB00011B/2379

* 9 7 8 0 9 9 9 0 6 7 1 0 9 *